Modern Indian Literature

Diaspora, Travel and Culture

Modern Indian Literature

Diaspora, Travel and Culture

Edited by

Sandeep Pathak

R.K. Dhawan

Prestige Books International

New Delhi

Published by
Prestige Books International
New Delhi 110 060
prestigebooks@gmail.com
Phone: 9818755529

Associate Office
P.O. Box 2250
Sydney 2001

ISBN: 978-81-947512-6-7

Printed in India

Contents

Introduction

Without literature, life is hell.

Charles Bukowski

The world of literature is a world where there is no reality except that of human imagination. The connection between literature and life is intimate and vital. Literature, it is said, is woven out of the stuff of life as mirror. Its significance depends on the depth and breadth of life that it paints. As life changes its contours, so does literature. Let us see, for example, how folklore has made inroads into Indian life and culture.

It is amazing that though the same stories are repeated over centuries, the stories do not lose their charm. The secret is in the satisfaction that our basic curiosity finds in the folktales. Listening to them, we marvel at the mysteries of the world and especially many inexplicable phenomena of universe around us. Through the folktales, we seem to be widening our horizon of life.

Contemporary literature reflects society's social, moral or political viewpoint. Writers in the present age look for themes that illuminate societal changes and weaknesses to remind society of the lessons they should learn and the questions they should ask. This process is not static. Since society changes over time, so do the themes and messages of the writers. Amitav Ghosh, for instance, is a modern writer whose literary creed and philosophy is contained almost entirely in his novels. He is greatly inspired by history and anthropology in the writing of his fiction. His quest for the past is characteristic of postmodernism.

It is commonly agreed that great literature grasps and reflects the changing conditions of social and moral life. It is essentially the outcome of creative thoughts and narrative skills. Poetry, drama, fiction and prose are the popular forms of literature. Literature has direct, exigent and spontaneous forms. It creates fascinating trends that shape our vision of life.

There is another school of thought. Some contemporary scholars tend to believe that the latest technology has adversely affected the tone and temper of literature. Facebook, blogging, twittering, instagram and the overuse of internet have reduced the importance of literature in the present times. But we must concede that such forms have come into vogue because of the popular demand and human needs. Earlier people used to write letters, diaries, and memoirs but now they have become a thing of the past. While there may be some loss of feeling and imagination, today's world is surely richer in words, ideas and concepts than the world that surrounded the primitive man.

Some art critics have derided the use of technology in our day-to-day life, as for them it impedes the flow of feeling and thought. Indeed every technological breakthrough is accompanied by the catastrophic effect on literature. Be it the arrival of TV, computer or smart phone. With the advent of tablets, e-books and computers, literature seems to have been relegated to the background. That is not the true picture. The new technologies produce new frameworks that adjust the ways in which literature appears: the page, the screen, the website, and the file window. Literature has the innate strength to demonstrate inventive capacity to adapt and evolve to new material conditions. It has changed the way we perceive, interpret, and even write literature. It has gained immensely in a multitude of different ways. More than anything else, it is providing a healthy discussion about the reception and understanding of literature.

(Dr.) Sandeep Pathak
Kanpur

(Dr.) R.K. Dhawan
New Delhi

India in Global Imagination

SUMITA PURI
Dyal Singh Evening College, University of Delhi

> The problem is not simply the "selfhood" of the nation as opposed to the "otherness" of other nations. We are confronted with the nation split within itself, articulating the heterogeneity of its population. (Homi K. Bhabha)

India, as imagined in the global context, is a complex and thought-provoking discursive space for research and deliberation. Literature is witness to the gamut of images, visions and emotions associated with India as a nation, as a figment of imagination or as a conceptual construct in the mind of writers as well as the readers. From the derogatory oriental tag—the land of mosquitoes, snake charmers, the adventurous and the mystic—to the land of fakirs, spirituality, the land of the golden bird and so forth, India has shouldered a colonial baggage of these acknowledged stereotypes, for writers across the globe, to interpret, examine, construct and finally deconstruct in the postcolonial era. The present paper reflects upon the heterogeneous ideological stances and re-presentations of India in the global imagination.

Let us begin with a discourse on whether India is a concept or a nation that is to be imagined by the writers inside/ outside India. Does India figure in the imaginative space or literary space or discursive space or exists as a geographically independent identity that encourages notions, expressions and narratives in the writer's imagination? Is India a nation independent of the imaginative eye or is it a concept derived from the re-presentations of the same in different historical periods? Does the India imagined by an Indian differ from the India imagined by an Indian no longer residing in India or the India in the Western writer's imagination? These are points of debate that attract scholars and intellectuals to state their opinions and viewpoints.

The West has loaded the Indian nation with its multifaceted connotations and nuances. On the one hand, India has been construed as a fissured and fragmented land based on its intrinsic hierarchical divisions of caste, class, gender and other marginalities. Yet, on the other hand, India is cognized as a united nation, in its struggle for independence against colonization. It has been glorified as a homogenized entity and yet appraised as a heterogeneous nation fighting within and without. It has been viewed as a land of cultural heritage, religious multiplicity, tribal songs, spiritualism along with being a land of bizarre landscapes and people. Apart from this communal, cultural and political extravaganza, fiction has depicted it as a nation filled with illiterate and uncouth population, whose life is governed by a corrupt and orthodox value system. All the same, the glorious past and the contemporary scenario in India picture in the efficacious yarns spun out of the imagination of writers inside/ outside India. India is a 'discursive formation' in these works, as Benedict Anderson defines the nation as an inevitable product of sociological factors such as common language, race, religion and history but also an "imagined political community—imagined as both inherently limited and sovereign." (6)

Whether critiqued or exalted, Aijaz Ahmad argues that any nation acquires specific meaning according to the socio-cultural context in which it is hypothesized: "My own view is that 'nation' is what is modern, especially so because, as a modern entity, it comes together with the making of a state—hence that hyphenated term 'nation-state.' However, nations are not conjured up out of emptiness; neither empty time, nor empty state. They arise, as outcomes of particular kinds of political projects, within a temporal continuum, and that continuum, which is the nation itself, is what we call (perhaps not very precisely 'the long past.'" (45)

Travellers and visitors from France, Italy and various parts of Asia, Africa or Europe have given their own labels; addressed India in their own terms, as per their experiences. The earliest representations of India can be seen in the works of Herodotus, for whom India was a wealthy and populous land. Hippocrates, on the other hand, contended that there is an 'inherent servility' in the people owing to the monarchical rule in India. The projection of the adventurous and exotic India was brought to the fore by Megasthenes who described the Holy River Ganges, the flora and fauna, and India as a land of spirituality practised by Brahmins and Fakirs. Travel to India in the Middle Ages led many writers to visualize it as a fabulous and opulent land. *The Travels of Sir John Mandeville*, *Gestes of Alexander* and *Romance of King Alysander* have cursory references to India. Marco Polo and Nicolo Conti refer to the religious rites but their tone is not one of condemnation.

On the one hand, these writers glorified the country for its populace and prosperity and yet the representations of merchant voyagers like the Russian Athanasius Nikitin, are irrefutably, (mis)representations: "All are black and wicked and the women all harlots or witches and they destroy their masters by poison" (Qtd. Oaten 41). Homi Bhabha in *The Location of Culture* elucidates that such negative stereotyping becomes problematic for the colonized nation to break away from and create new representations in the psyche of the people: "The stereotype is not a simplification because it is false representation of a given reality. It is simplification because it is an arrested, fixated form of representation that in denying the play of difference [that the negation through the other permits] constitutes a problem for the representation of the subject in signification of psychic and social relations." (Qtd. Menon 17)

Visitors to the Mughal court recorded their views about the judiciary, administration, material prosperity and religious rituals of that era. Having painted too rosy a picture of the Orient, writers like Edward Terry sneered at India, lest it is too eulogized in the British eye: "Lest this remote country should seem like an earthly paradise without any discommodities, very great was the danger there from lions, tigers, and jackals in the rivers from crocodiles and on the land from snakes and other venomous and pernicious beasts." (Qtd. Forster 123)

With the advent of the colonial ruler, India's glory and wealth had been looted, impressions of which are manifested in the literature of the epoch. The imperial annexations and the resultant stereotyping of the East became fixated in the minds of the writers for years to come. Images such as 'the land of snake charmers' drawn by writers like E.M. Forster are monolithic, derogatory and highly subjective. Having carried the white man's burden on its shoulder for long, unable to remove the colonial tag, India has been ever struggling to free itself from the clutches of Eurocentrism. And yet, with the onset of neo-colonialism, it has been, once again, fettered in new chains.

The conflict between tradition and modernity came to be voiced in the writings of Indian novelists in the post-independence times. Bankim Chandra Chatterjee's *Rajmohan's Wife: A Novel*, considered as the first Indian English novel, attracted the Western reader for its dexterous analysis of the urban middle class's psychological and social woes. Toru Dutt, Michael Madhusudan Dutt, Lal Bihari Dey, Sardar Jogendra Singh and others, belonging to the first generation of Indian English novelists, picked up socio-cultural and historical motifs to be recognized in the literary arena. The fiction of the 'Big Three' of Indian English fiction—R.K. Narayan, Raja Rao and Mulk Raj Anand—invoked the traditional India with its cultural and religious legacy. The hegemonic colonial rule, the Gandhian discourse, the hierarchical positions of caste and class in India were served with Indian English flavour for the reader to savour and cherish. R.K. Narayan's novels are mostly set in the fictional village of Malgudi, and illustrate the rural India with his witty disposition. *Swami and Friends, The Financial Expert, The Vendor of Sweets, The Bachelor of Arts* are some of his best-known works. Gandhi as a major motif figures distinctly in his *Waiting for the Mahatma* followed by Raja Rao's *Kanthapura.* Employing the Western form of the stream of consciousness and the dramatic monologue, the novel and its creator, fervently posit the need for Indians to write in the colonial lingo. Raja Rao's literary corpus includes *The Serpent and the Rope*, *The Cat and Shakespeare, Comrade Kirillov* and *The Chessmaster and His Moves*. Oppression based on caste and class are at the core of Mulk Raj Anand's novels such as *Untouchable, Coolie, Two Leaves and a Bud* and *The Sword and the Sickle.* His protagonists demonstrate their anguish and rebel against the structured social evils prevalent in India of those times.

Bhabani Bhattacharya's *So many Hungers!*, Khushwant Singh's *Train to Pakistan* and *Delhi*, Ahmed Ali's *Twilight in Delhi*, Attia Hosain's *Sunlight on a Broken Column* are poignant portrayals of the Indian independence movement and its aftermath. Post-independence, India has evolved as a pluralistic, multicultural and multi-ethnic nation-state in the writings of Indian English authors. The rendition of the hybrid Indian identity is coupled with an experimentation with the formal aspects as well, seen palpably in the works like Salman Rushdie's *Midnight's Children,* and *Haroun and the Sea of Stories,* Amitav Ghosh's *Shadow Lines* and *The Sea of Poppies,* Vikram Seth's *The Golden Gate* and *A Suitable Boy* and Shashi Tharoor's *The Great Indian Novel.* The celebrated women writers have ranged from Nayantara Sahgal, who shot to fame with *Rich like Us*, Anita Desai, who became popular for her *Fire on the Mountain* along with her daughter Kiran Desai with *The Inheritance of Loss* to Arundhati Roy who bagged the Booker for *The God of Small Things*, Shashi

Deshpande for her *That Long Silence* and Jhumpa Lahiri for *Interpreter of Maladies* and *The Namesake.*

The manifestation of the Indian reality is expressed in the genres of poetry and drama as well. The poetry of the trail-blazers Rabindranath Tagore, Toru Dutt, Michael Madhusudan Dutt, Sarojini Naidu, Derozio and others, along with the prominent Nissim Ezekiel, Kamala Das, A.K. Ramanujan, Jayanta Mahapatra and the contemporary Keki N. Daruwalla, Shiv K. Kumar and A.N. Dwivedi explores the individual crisis pitted against the social one from the colonial to the modern period in Indian history. The Nava rasa ascribed to 'the fifth veda' by Bharata is affirmed as the origin of drama in India. However, Indian drama in English evolved much later with the plays of Michael Madhusudan Dutt, Sri Aurobindo and Rabindranath Tagore. Harindranath Chattopadhyay, Bharati Sarabhai and J.M. Lobo Prabhu and Nissim Ezekiel paved the way for the later dramatists like Girish Karnad, Vijay Tendulkar, Badal Sircar and Mahasweta Devi to experiment with form and content through the juxtaposition of tradition and modernity.

The writers's choice to write against the European dominance in the colonial language is conditioned by the urge to reach out to a transnational reader. The Caribbean poet Derek Walcott portrays this dilemma in "A Far Cry from Africa":

> Where shall I turn, divided to the vein?
> I who have cursed
> The drunken officer of British rule, how choose
> Between this Africa, and the English tongue I love?
> Betray them both, or give back, what they give? (Breslin 62)

This position is essentially in contrast to the political stand of writers like Ngugi wa Thiong'o, who encourage writers to make their native language their linguistic choice: "the real language that one is looking for is the language of struggle, the language of transformation of our various societies. And eventually this language can only be found in the action and feeling and thoughts and experiences of the working people."

Colonialism also led to mass migration of indentured labour to the West. Generations to follow faced inequity of all sorts creating 'imaginary homelands' in their minds, to borrow Rushdie's lexis. The yearning to return coupled with the desire to fit in in the new milieu made writers of the Diaspora to imagine India in their own subjective ways. While some dealt with the nostalgia along with the loss of culture and identity, others embraced the new multicultural chiselled identity either in the melting pot of United States of America or in the multicultural mosaic of Canada. For some, it became a getaway from the religious, political and socio-cultural muddle that exists in India. On the other hand, India figured in the memoirs and imaginative space of writers suffering the angst of homelessness. Bill Ashcroft expounds: "More importantly perhaps, diasporic writing, in its crossing of borders, opens up the horizon of place. What does 'home' mean in the disrupted world of colonial space? How can 'home' become the transformative habitation of boundaries? Ironically, one of the consequences of the disruptions and displacements of colonization has been that 'home,' like 'place,' becomes freed from a simple spatial concept of location. It occupies time as well as space; it becomes a way of seeing, a way of inhabiting and, ultimately, a way of transforming global discourses of power by being 'at home' in them" (131). Diasporic writers from South Asia settled abroad have dealt with all of this and much more in their fiction, drama and poetry. Rohinton Mistry, Farrukh Dhondy, Firdaus Kanga, Salman Rushdie, V.S. Naipaul, Suniti Namjoshi, Uma Parameswaran, Shauna Singh Baldwin, Meera Syal, Rana Bose, Anita Rau Badami, Bharati Mukherjee, Sunetra Gupta, Chitra Banerjee Divakaruni and many others paint their own pictures of India for the readers worldwide. Women writers depict the displacement of women in a 'Trishanku' like state, borrowing Uma Parameswaran's title. History, culture, loss, the socio-psychological debacle, the Indian individual as well as the community create the culturally diverse 'Bhaji' on the 'Beach' and, thus, are at the crux of Indian diasporic writing.[1]

The formulation of India poses another pronounced challenge: for whom are these writers writing? Is the image of India imagined in their constructed narratives for themselves or for the unfamiliar reader? Potent accounts of the historical struggles of India, the re-telling of myths, tales, legends and allegories, the culturally rich heritage and so on in the fiction of writers of Indian origin settled abroad corroborate the urgency to bind themselves to their roots as well as to share these images with the non-Indian readers. At the same time, the contemporary postcolonial and neo-colonial writer resolves to fight and write back to the empire; to subvert the Indian identity created by the Occidental pen; to re-write her/his own rendering of the given from the Oriental perspective.

Thus, while addressing the global reader, about the India imagined or envisioned, a writer becomes obliged to address issues of race, caste, class, gender, politics and religion. Colonialism, partition and other significant events in the history of India are popular leitmotifs—hinted at subtly or as the major tropes of the story. Nationalism in Rabindranath Tagore's *The Home and the World* or Amitav Ghosh's *The Shadow Lines* are relevant examples to substantiate the aforesaid viewpoint. Eventually, it is either the notion of India the writer wants to envisage or the India the reader wants to know about. As Pi refutes in *Life of Pi* by Yann Martel, when the two Japanese insurance agents come to interview him: "I know what you want. . . . You need a story that won't surprise you. That will confirm what you already know" (336). Thus, the writers supplying the varied models of India available to their all-inclusive readers confront the dilemma of countering these existing models provided by the Western writer and consequently re-constitute their own models.

The present-day Indian authors have a panorama of themes to address with their subjective ideologies—social, cultural, religious and political. The young literary talents weave composite innovative tales, complex characters and metanarratives. The compulsions of history, westernization, modernity, globalization and the Indian political turbulence on the Indian individual losing his culture and traditions are dealt by writers like Amit Chaudhari in works like *The Immortals* and *A New World,* Upamanyu Chatterjee in *English, August: An Indian Story,* Jhumpa Lahiri in her *The Lowland,* Aravind Adiga in *The White Tiger* and *Last Man in Tower*, Jeet Thayil in *Narcopolis*, Chitra Banerjee Divakaruni in *The Mistress of Spices,* Manju Kapur in *Difficult Daughters*, Keki N. Daruwalla in *Love across the Salt Desert* and *Ancestral Affairs* and many more. The cult of the globalized Indian in a multicultural scenario can be witnessed in the popular bestsellers like Chetan Bhagat's *One Night at the Call Centre, 2 States*, Anuja Chauhan's *Those Pricey Thakur Girls,* Chitra Banerjee Divakaruni's *The Vine of Desire* and the refreshing works of Yashodhara Lal like *Just Married, Please Excuse* and *There's Something about You* and yet the fiction of Amish Tripathi, Devdutt Pattanaik and Anant Pai revisit Indian mythology and folklore. Gender oppression in the fiction of Sudha Murthy and Anita Nair is supported by the bold expression of Shobha De and Kamala Das.

The discussion, thus, brings us back to the quintessential question: Is India a nation-state independent of the sundry visions of its writers—Indian/ Non-Indian or is India a notion, an 'imaginary homeland,' an 'imagined community' perceived by the writers?[2] Is there a single 'India' or 'Many Indias' and consequentially an 'India' in the global imagination or 'Many Indias and Many Literatures'[3] discernible to the global reader? The writer, today, thus, bears the brunt of contemplating, conceptualizing, theorizing, and interpreting the coercive forces operational in the Indian society; to re-present her/ his India to the world. To conclude in the words of Helen Tiffin: "Not surprisingly, it is representation—the ways in which we represent ourselves to ourselves and to 'outsiders'—which sustains and sometimes even constructs our nations, providing us with the very basis of communal identification. Accounts of heroic struggles against foreign incursion; inter-generational recounting of national myths and legends; the (re)invention of the past; the writing and reading of ancient and modern allegories; the sharing of emotive symbols such as flags and emblems, are but a few of the various forms of representation which maintain the powerful fiction of the nation." (21-22)

NOTES

1. *Bhaji on the Beach* is a British comedy drama film scripted by Meera Syal and directed by Gurinder Chadha.
2. For a detailed study refer to *Imaginary Homelands* by Salman Rushdie, *Imagined Communities: Reflections on the Origin and Spread of Nationalism* by Benedict Anderson.
3. The title is borrowed from *Many Indias, Many Literatures: New Critical Essays* by Shormishtha Panja.

Works Cited

Anderson, Benedict. *Imagined Communities: Reflections on the Origin and Spread of Nationalism.* London and New York: Verso, 1991.

Bhabha, Homi K. *The Location of* Culture. London: Routledge, 1994.

Breslin, Paul. *Nobody's Nation: Reading Derek Walcott.* Chicago and London: The University of Chicago Press, 2001.

Dhawan, R.K. et al, ed. *India in Canadian Imagination: A Literary Response.* New Delhi: Prestige, 2003.

Forster, William, ed. *Early Travels in India 1583-1619.* London: OUP, 1921.

Martel, Yann. *Life of Pi.* Toronto: Random House, 2001.

Menon, Sindhu. *Images of Colonial India in British Writing: 1757-1857.* New Delhi: Prestige, 2008.

Oaten, E.F. *European Travellers in India.* New Delhi: Asian Educational Services, 1991.

Panja, Shormishtha, ed. *Many Indias, Many Literatures: New Critical Essays.* New Delhi: Worldview, 1999.

Parameswaran, Uma. *Trishanku and Other Writings.* New Delhi: Prestige, 1998.

Rushdie, Salman. *Imaginary Homelands: Essays and Criticism 1981-1991.* The University of Michigan: Granta, 1992.

Said, Edward W. *Orientalism: Western Conceptions of the Orient.* Harmondsworth: Penguin, 1995.

Thiong'o, Ngugi wa, "The Language of Struggle," *Transition,* 54, 1991, 142-54.

Vijayasree et al, ed. *Nation in Imagination: Essays on Nationalism, Sub-Nationalisms and Narration*. India: Orient Longman, 2007.

Nation, Nationalism and Transnationalism in Amitav Ghosh's Novels: A Study

MEETU BHATIA KAPUR
Vivekananda Instt. of Professional Studies, I.P. Univ., Delhi

The growth of industrialization promoted travel writing quite exponentially. Every fiction writer of consequence from Defoe to Addison to Fielding and Smollett, Johnson, Boswell, and Sterne in the eighteenth century produced one overt travel book. They use the knowledge of an immense range of geographic, historical, cultural, scientific and sometimes mystical element in their works to revise and transform generic conventions and produce a polyphonic mode of travel writing.

Globalization comes to be widely re-defined in the works of the writers closely working on the travel writings. Diaspora writing in this context covers a large deal of historical and cultural perspectives. Traversing through the past to explore the future, is the prime concern of the travel writers. The geographical territories not only capture the psychological phenomena of the characters but also define the spatial constituents of the characters and locations respectively.

The spirit of nationalism glows through the writings involving travel writings. This is easily justified in the works of a variety of writers like Richard Burton, Peter Martyn and on the home front Amitav Ghosh, Jhumpa Lahiri and much more alike. The territories both in national and international form reset the world order. Topics like politics, kingship, warfare, national and international racial temperaments, religion, custom, tradition and other country based issues dominate the writings of these writers.

Nation, nationalism, and transnationalism is widely covered in the novels of Amitav Ghosh. His writings strike the readers as a mirror of the past and a peep into the future. He is able to connect with the readers because of the intense connection of societal and cultural effects. The life of Ghosh is a testimony of a transnationalism upbringing. Born and brought up in Calcutta, his formative years were spent in Bangladesh, Sri Lanka and India. His education took him to Oxford, then to Delhi before finally settling down in New York. Journey, boundaries, and territories constitute the major portion in his work. The shadow of Egypt, Dhaka, Israeli, East Africa and Calcutta are some unmistakably a reflection of cross country writings. Every land is renamed, remapped and reclaimed in his writings. Every angle of his work largely aims at landscaping the interior and exterior aspect i.e. it is not only physical but also mental. With every country, an emotion or a feeling is linked.

Temporal with the spatial boundaries evokes the boundlessness of the inner being, its wide range of emotional repertoires in these given frames. By calling attention to the imagining of nations as bounded territorial space, Ghosh opens out possibilities of other imagination as well.

Movement in all aspects and conditions—historical, geographical, cultural—gives a framework to Amitav Ghosh's works. To a very large extent, his fiction has a continuous changing, evolving ambience. The feeling of locatedness and dislocation hangs like a pendulum throughout his novels. On one hand, the locatedness executes a sense of warm security, a feeling of permanence as opposed to the sense of chaotic upheaval that its part, counter dislocation brings. His work expands cognitively, culturally, as a trope that evinces a multi-layeredness, which encapsulates geographical, psychological and cultural space. This establishes Amitav Ghosh as a modern writer who handles history and cradles it into the present scenario. What political lines divide, his writings unite. The historical moments accompanied by a cultural and psychological travelling gives a different genre to his novels.

His first novel *The Circle of Reason* (1980) attempted to write a new history from a novelist standpoint. This novel depicts the border and the crossing of the borderland. The writer brings together both Indian and Western elements, thus making even the title suggestive.

The elements which make the title in sync with the theme of nationalism and internationalism are the three gunas i.e. *Satwa, Rajas* and *Tamas* where *Satwa* is a western concept associated with reason and has the power to think rationally, a scientific way of discriminating between right and wrong, a state minus superstition, progressive attitude and civilized way of life. The writer brings together both Indian and Western elements, thus making even the title suggestive. Ironically, as the characters move towards the West, passion and death dominate. The second guna 'Rajas: Passion' has an outward movement. Rajas is an impurity which leads to action. In this section, the Rajas people indulge in talking, telling, listening, gossiping, fighting, falling prey to conspiracies, dancing, worrying about things. All the pandemonium created at the end of the section "*Rajas*: Passion," prepares us for the final section of the novel called "*Tamas*: Death." *Tamas* is described as "Darkness and Inertia": "Besides this, Tamas also indicates a tendency to decay and to die. In a little lawn of Et Oued on the north-eastern edge of the Algerian Sahara Carbolic acid is converted into Ganga Jal to purify the corpse of Kulfi. Dr. Mishra wonders in the small town of desert: 'The world has come full circle.'" (411)

As the characters move towards the West, passion and death dominate. Initially the novel covers a refugee village, with reference to Bangladesh and Calcutta, finally moving to the Middle East via Kerala. Neither entirely rural nor urban and with no stable idea of attitude, it becomes an epic of restlessness. This is typical of travel narrative crossing the boundaries of one nation and moving to the next. Focusing on a motley group of migrants drawn from various parts of India on an imaginary island al-Ghazira and then Algeria, the novel marks the search for the meaningfulness of those whose lives are displaced by globalization and whose very bodies bear the violent marks of history. The vision of globalization: it gives readers a sense of the different lives, motives, and aspirations. The journey as a motif runs throughout the novel and unites its three parts. Characters cross borders "with almost the biological necessity if not always the ease and no chance of migratory birds." This motif is particularly associated with the one who is on the run having been branded extremist by the police and with Jyoti Das close on his heels always. He moves from Lalpukar to Kerala and then sets off to al-Ghazira in the Middle East along with a number of characters who travel in search of material wealth and more opportunities. Travel itself is converted into a homeland. For Jyoti Das, more than the professional obligations, it was the prospect of seeing more kinds on his travels that urges him to move on in his pursuit of Alu. Ironically it was he who causes the journey al-Ghazira through Alexandria, Egypt, Lisbon, Junis to the little town of Et Oved. *The Circle of Reason* enables the articulation of the kind of transnational feminist practice which we need. Ghosh's novels reverberate the forms of violence that nationality and globalization manifest in the home, in domestic spaces, and in private lives.

The Shadow Lines (1988) takes the narrative beyond the national frontiers and opens out the narrative to encompass experiences that are cosmopolitan and unfolds itself against the mood and background of a new internationalism. There is a search for invisible links ranging across the realities of nationality, cultural segregation, and social discrimination. The author questions the validity of the geographical boundaries and celebrates the union of allies pulled together by self-propelling empathy and attachment. Economic social, cultural and intellectual freedom is well-encompassed in *The Shadow Lines* by exploring connections, distinctions, and possibilities. Amitav Ghosh very articulately creates a changing world with different strands of nationalism and ideology. He shows how different cultures and communities are becoming a major issue in contemporary India. The author realizes that with the dominant tradition as the only legitimate source of India's complex culture, communal antagonism will grow. He effectively uses political allegory to stress the need for a syncretism civilization, to avoid a communal holocaust. The main storyline gets connected to a number of other global events. He evokes postcolonial situations, cultural dislocations, and anxieties in the period between 1962 and 1979 and interprets the issues of fractured nationalists in close and telling encounters. The narrator, with his expanded horizons and imaginative understanding of the world, caught in the vortex of violence and murderous rampage, stresses on the urgency of preserving the memories of saner and humane transaction for cultural self-determination and inter-personal communication. It focuses on Ghosh's treatment of the changing middle-class ethos in India during the pre- and post-Independence era. The lines of the characters in this novel are determined largely by their idea of freedom and this idea, in its turn, is shaped by the history of the times.

There are several lines of the family introduced—that of the narrator based in Calcutta; that of his grandmother's sister, associated with Dhaka and two further lines bringing into story Robi and Ila. The unnamed closest links are with Mayadebi, his grandmother's sister, and with her son, the enigmatic older friend through which the narrator experiences much of his life. Amitav Ghosh shows that in a changing world different strands of nationalism and ideology will exist and even compete. The force of nationalism in the quest for freedom or ideology is often a source of violence—so the shadow line between people and nation is often a mere illusion. The force and appeal of nationalism cannot be crushed so easily, just as death by a communal mob in the bylanes of Old Dhaka. Her memories were like falcon rising from the depths of despair, literally from the proverbial ashes. Her tender reminiscences about her happy days of childhood and the heart-break of the disintegration of their joint family are vividly transmitted through her imagination and memory. It captures the young narrator's imagination and makes it a living experience. The grandmother's visit of her ancestral home is one of the most memorable scenes in English fiction. Before flying to Dhaka she asks her son if she would be able "to see the border between India and East Pakistan from the plane." (151) In the course of conversation, Tha'mma ends up questioning some of the fundamentals of her idea of nationalism: "But if there aren't any trenches or anything, how are people to know? I mean, where's the difference then? And if there's no difference both the sides will be the same; it'll be just like it used to be before, when we used to catch a train in Dhaka and get off in Calcutta the next day, without stopping us what was it for all then—the partition and the killing and everything—is there isn't anything in between." (151)

In an Antique Land (1992) hits the readers as a major travelogue. It discusses the intricate problems of the characters associated with migration. History and imagination are indivisibly and inextricably linked in this work. It points out the tragic turn of events in the history of Asia and the Middle East and particularly India. The main focus of the novel is on the unarmed nature of Indian trade and commerce before the advent of Vasco-de-Gama in India; on the forgotten period of history showing free and liberal India's collaboration with Arab and Chinese world and an easy flow of warmth and trust which existed between Tunisian Jewish merchant and his Indian helper Bomma.

The book establishes Amitav Ghosh not just as a writer of fiction, but also a keen traveller, a diligent researcher, a social anthropologist and a social historian. It is an interaction of the author with at least four languages and cultures spread across continents and centuries. He uses history to bring Egypt close to India by setting up a series of exchanges between different interactive sites located across the two countries. He maps some of the trade routes between India and Egypt via the Mediterranean; compares the cosmopolitan settlements on the Malabar Coast with hybrid Jewish communities in Egypt and shows how names are cross-fertilized when they travel across nations and acquire new forms elsewhere. But something happens to the quality of this interaction when we move from the canvas of history to the present time. Two cultures confront each other across an insurmountable gap created by mutual incomprehension. Cultural symbols painstakingly decoded by historical analysis suddenly become opaque in the context of fieldwork interaction. Names and places become symbols of cultural hybridity and exchange. Modern man in the contemporary scenario is facing the ghost of alienation in a different context. Just like the seventieth century, England people from the third world developed countries like India, Pakistan and Bangladesh have been migrating to the developing countries, but when this success proves to be an illusion, disillusionment descends. A foreign nation remains a foreign land for them; however hard they try they cannot break away from their roots back home. Thus, they face alienation. This theme of emigration leading to alienation is elaborated in the character of Ben Yiju who in the very beginning of the novel is described thus: "A Jewish merchant, originally of Tunisia, who had gone to India by the way of Egypt, as a trader and had spent seventeen years there. A man of many accomplishments, a distinguished calligrapher, scholar and poet, Ben, Yiju had returned to Egypt having amassed great wealth in India." (19) This creates a unified and brilliantly arranged story. *The Shadow Lines* is a prelude to *In an Antique Land*. The thought process which starts in *The Shadow Lines* reaches its culmination in this novel.

The novel completes its circle with different sections called 'Lataifa,' 'Nashaway,' 'Mangalore' and 'Going Back,' with Prologue and Epilogue completing the theme. Every section has some theme to offer. The first three sections deal with the social and cultural history of Egypt. 'Mangalore' deals with Ben Yiju's stay in India for seventeen years. The last section is a summing up of the novelist's search for Ben Yiju's life and through him his search for cultural and political changes. The prologue of the novel contains the gist of the novel.

> I was a student, twenty-two years old, and I had recently won a scholarship awarded by the foundation established by a family of expatriate Indians. It was only a few months since I had left India so I was little more baffled by my situation than students usually are. At that moment the only thing I knew about my future was that I was expected to do research leading towards the doctorate in social anthropology. I had never heard of the Cairo Genira before that day, but within a few months, I was in Tunisia learning Arabic. At about the same time the next year, 1980, I was in Egypt installed in a village called Lataifa, a couple of house journey to the south-east of Alexandria. (19)

The novel ends with questions like: Why wars? Have we learned any lesson from history? What is the aim of our life? What are we looking for: peace, comfort or happiness? What is the meaning of civilization? The novel also offers vivid glimpses of the many small, indistinguishable, intertwined histories—Indian and Egyptian, Muslim and Jewish, Hindu and Muslim—which prevailed until some centuries ago, but which then became partitioned in several areas where they had once existed. *In an Antique Land* thus is a travel book which records people and their manners.

The hybridity of Indian English with its richness and complexities of Indian culture has won wide audiences in a globalized world. Amitav Ghosh combines innovation of postmodern fiction with an insight to produce powerful and provocative investigations of the postcolonial world. Each of his novels is a "mapping test" which explores the cultural and societal effects of changing sense of time and place. The outscape gets inscaped, i.e., not only the exterior territories are mapped, but also the inner recesses of the mind. The feeling of nationalism and yearning for one's motherland are accompanied by a feeling of warmth, security and chaotic upheaval. This multi-layeredness encapsulates geographical, psychological and cultural space. Salman Rushdie calls this form of writing *a historical weightlessness.* The history is revisited, re-explored and the residual effects of politics are re-exposed leading to colonizing the landscape to knowing the gaze or privileged point of view of its indigenous population.

Works Cited

Ghosh, Amitav. *The Shadow Lines*. Ravi Dayal, 1988.
_____. *In An Antique Land*. Ravi Dayal, 1992.
_____. *Circle of Reason*. Mariner Books, 1986.

Travels and Travails: Women in Amitav Ghosh's *Gun Island*

RITA JOSHI
Lady Shri Ram College, University of Delhi

Amitav Ghosh's fiction centres around the migration of people across the ages which he sees as a defining characteristic of human experience. Ghosh's novels dwell in 'cultures that flow across boundaries" (Dixon 10). *Gun Island* (2019), too, focuses on travel across nations by various characters—in the past, in the legend of the Gun Merchant who came to Venice from the Sunderbans for trade, in the present the travels of Deen between the Sunderbans, Venice and the U.S. as he researches into the legend of the Gun Merchant. Cinta, a scholar, travels to Calcutta to research on historical ties of trade between Venice and Bengal.

Women occupy a central place in *Gun Island.* In Ghosh's earlier novels women have played a part but are more acted upon than agents of destiny. We recall traditional elderly women like Toru-Debi in *The Circle of Reason* (1986) and the narrator's grandmother in *The Shadow Lines* (1988). There are women who are exploited migrant labour like Zindi in *The Circle of Reason* and Deeti in *Sea of Poppies* (2008). *Gun Island* presents us with women who are self-possessed and agents of their own and others' destinies. Many of these women are intellectuals and scholars and Ghosh forefronts such women in this novel. It is almost a statement about the great contribution of women to contemporary forays into knowledge and culture. Cinta, Piya and Lisa are scholars while Gisella is a filmmaker; Lubna in Venice and Nilima in the

Sunderbans are activists engaged in aiding the homeless and migrants.

A central female character is the wrathful goddess, Manasa Devi, who figures as a trope in the novel and also provides a basis for the plot which concerns itself with the travels of Deen in search of material about the Gun Merchant and Manasa Devi. Hindu goddesses come in two varieties, the benign and the wrathful. Manasa Devi, goddess of snakes, belongs to the latter category:

> Manasa enjoys a widespread cult as a deity, mostly in Bengal, where she is invoked for protection against snakebites, as curer of diseases and bringer of wealth. . . . She is probably of pre-Aryan origin and the best-known myth about her concerns the way in which she forced recognition for herself. Manasa grew angry with a rich merchant named Chand, . . . She demanded his worship . . . he refused. . . . She capsized his ships containing all his wealth and left him far from home, a castaway (Ions 99).

In the novel the legend of the goddess traverses different locales. She is shown harming the merchant even in Venice. The conflict between the goddess and the merchant becomes a conflict between nature and man, goodness and greed. In a talk at the release of his book in Delhi in June 2019, Ghosh stated that the merchant "was a trope for trade" The merchant and the goddess dramatize "the conflict between profit and the world" (Joshi 98).

Manasa Devi pursued the Gun Merchant in the form of poisonous reptiles, scorpions and suchlike which bit the merchant time and again. In the novel the merchant is supposed to have been bitten by a spider in Venice. Like characters in the novel Manasa Devi and her retinue of animals are present in different countries. The labourer, Rafi, is convinced he sees the goddess in Venice.

Trade and the lure of wealth caused the Gun Merchant to come to Venice. In the modern era refugees from Bangladesh travel to Venice as illegal immigrants for profit. Transporting these labourers provides a huge profit for middlemen in several countries. Snakes and creatures associated with Manasa Devi appear in different locales in the novel—the principle of nature's war against corrupt humans is evident in the twentieth century.

When Deen visits the shrine of Manasa Devi in the Sunderbans he confronts a huge king cobra. It does not strike Deen who is a simple, good man engaged in the pursuit of knowledge. The cobra strikes Tipu who has been corrupted by the West. A snake appears in L.A. killing a dog. Bark beetles eat up barks of trees in forests near L.A. which become like firewood and there are wild forest fires during the drought. Deen sees a spider in Venice. Cinta is bitten by shipworms.

In Venice Manasa Devi morphs into a more benign counterpart—Mary, mother of Jesus. Cinta tells Deen of a seventeenth century legend (at about the time Manasa Devi is supposed to have persecuted the Gun Merchant). Plague spread over Italy at this time. One girl placed a painting of the Madonna over her door. It is believed the plague never entered that alley. A church was built there to the Madonna of Good Health parallelling the shrine to Manasa Devi in the Sunderbans.

A female character in the novel prominent as any male is Cinta. She befriends Deen. She helps him with his research and offers him moral and emotional support. She travels to Calcutta to research historic trade ties between Venice and Bengal. Deen and she travel to and fro between Calcutta and Venice in pursuit of their separate researches.

Though Cinta has faced personal tragedy in the untimely death of her husband and daughter in a car accident, she is strong and carries on undefeated with her work. She is a renowned research scholar and speaker. Her interest in the medieval spice trade to Venice brings her to Calcutta. Deen thinks: "it seemed wonderfully original to me that someone should want to travel to India to study the history of Venice" (30).

She has an interest in folklore as a valid form of knowledge though Deen is rational and a sceptic. She describes 'tarantism,' a form of dancing and exorcism of spirits. She tells Deen: "to say that you don't believe in the 'supernatural' is a contradiction in terms—because it means that you also don't believe in the 'natural.' Neither can exist without the other" (35). She speaks of foreknowledge and the ancient Aztec predictions where they intuitively knew that invaders would come across the seas one day wearing helmets and carrying fire (37). Highlighting the value of folklore, Cinta states:

> In the seventeenth century no one would have ever said of something that it was 'just a story' as we moderns do. At that time people recognized that stories could tap into dimensions that were beyond the ordinary, beyond the human even. They knew that only through stories was it possible to enter the most inward mysteries of our existence. . . . Only through stories can invisible or inarticulate or silent beings speak to us. (127)

In giving credibility to folklore as a valid form of history or knowledge, Cinta highlights the focus of Ghosh in this novel on the links between myth and history as demonstrated in the legend of Manasa Devi and the Gun Merchant. Ghosh's interests as an anthropologist colour his fictional imagination and concerns in the novel.

Three women who first appeared in Ghosh's earlier novel, *The Hungry Tide* (2008) reappear in this novel. These are Nilima, Moyna and Piya: "Nilima, Moyna and Piya are women in control of their lives. . . . They contribute to the survival and welfare of the community" (Mukerji 325).

Nilima runs the Badabon Trust, an NGO, in the Sunderbans. She has been defiant of society. Though she comes from a wealthy Calcutta family, she marries an impoverished schoolteacher and moves to Lusibari in the Sunderbans. The Badabon Trust is a charitable organization which runs free schools and hospitals in the area. Nilima is instrumental in introducing Deen to Piya in *Gun Island.*

Moyna's story is given in detail in *Hungry Tide.* She is an educated nurse who marries a displaced victim of the Morijhapi massacre. He is killed when he rescues Piya from a cyclonic storm. Moyna is a self-reliant woman who continues to work and support herself and her son. However, in *Gun Island* her son, Tipu, is taken by Piya to the U.S. and he becomes increasingly alienated from his mother. Moyna in this novel represents the abandoned group of women whose husbands and sons travel abroad for work usually as illegal immigrants.

Piya is a cetologist. She is a Westernized Indian domiciled in Oregon, U.S. She frequently travels to the Sunderbans to study river dolphins. She is fiercely concerned about the threat to them from pollutants from a factory which empties its waste into the river. Piya receives threats from the villagers for trying to stop the factory as it will lead to loss of jobs. She invites a journalist and a photographer to accompany her to witness a 'beaching' when hundreds of dolphins leave the polluted river and come on its banks and die of asphyxiation. She hopes to use the report and photographs of the journalist to spread awareness about the plight of the dolphins and to get an order from the Supreme Court to stop the factory.

Piya's main failure is as foster mother to Moyna's son, Tipu. She takes him to the U.S. He becomes alienated from his home context and does not fit into life in the Sunderbans on his return. Piya gifts Tipu laptops, phones, music systems. When Tipu complains he cannot use the gadgets due to power cuts she has the house solarized. But as a result of Piya's misplaced generosity, Moyna and Tipu find themselves "in a bubble of affluence within the increasingly impoverished terrain that they actually inhabited" (60). Further, Piya does not know anything about child-raising: "it was not as if she had a family, or knew anything about bringing up children" (80-81).

As a result Tipu falls in with the wrong group of youngsters and has brushes with the police. Piya now returns him to his mother. He can no longer go to the ordinary school in Lusibari and is put in an expensive school in Calcutta from where he is expelled. He refuses to study and ends up as an illegal immigrant to Venice. Despite her good intentions Piya is responsible for the deteriorating trajectory of Tipu as she failed to see the impact of transnational travel on a poor immigrant boy.

Towards the end of the novel Piya offers the ageing Deen the possibility of a romantic partnership. She invites him to live with her in Oregon. Piya, too, seems to be ready to move out of her reclusive lifestyle and this possible partnership provides the novel with an element of hope.

Several minor women characters add to the concerns of the novel. Gisella is an openly gay woman. Ghosh touches upon another kind of liberated woman in the person of Gisella. She lives with her female partner. She is an activist who makes documentary films which are social comments. She and her girlfriend have adopted two refugee children. She makes a documentary on the refugees coming in the Blue Boat to Venice and the hostile reception of the authorities. She hopes the film will bring public awareness of the plight of refugees.

Lubna is a migrant Bangladeshi woman in Venice who works for the refugees there. She tells Deen: "I feel responsible for these boys. They've no one else to turn to" (158). Rafi tells Deen that Lubna teaches the refugees their rights under the law and so helps them regain their confidence and become assertive. Like Nilima is a protective mother figure to the poor in Lusibari, Lubna is a protective mother-figure to the poor in Venice. Both recall the Madonna of Good Health in Venice (discussed above).

Another scholarly woman who is also an activist is Lisa. She is an entomologist who lives in Los Angeles. She is engaged in the study of bark beetles who eat up trees from the inside so that when the weather turns dry they are like dead wood and easily catch fire causing forest fires. Lisa tries to warn the authorities but they pay no heed to her warnings and treat her as a nosy outsider. There is a huge fire. The town is not grateful to her and accuses her of starting the fire herself to gain attention and prove her point.

Lisa, an earnest scientist, is disregarded by a patriarchal society. She receives death threats in Los Angeles for her environmental concerns as did Piya in the Sunderbans: "It's like we're back in the Dark Ages—women being attacked as witches" (109).

Very different to these scholarly, educated women—and perhaps included in the novel as a contrast to them—are a group of women in the Sunderbans who are sex workers. They have been rounded up by the police from various red-light districts in Kolkata. They were originally from the Sunderbans and have been sent back there to be rehabilitated with the help of the Badabon Trust. But the Trust cannot help them much financially so they return to the city and continue as sex workers. The plight of the labour class in the novel including these sex workers and the illegal immigrants to Venice is grim.

A discussion of the female characters in the novel would not be complete without the mention of the dolphin, Rani. Rani is a matriarchal protector of her pod. Piya had known Rani's mother and there is a sense of a relationship between Piya and Rani: "Rani was now the oldest living member of the pod and a true matriarch" (92). When the river becomes very polluted Rani leads her pod to safer waters.

There is a comparison made between the stress of the displaced dolphins and displaced villagers in the Sunderbans: "Rani and her pod . . . it's been a huge source of stress for them . . . Moyna said something similar when she was talking about the people who're leaving the Sunderbans" (97). The dolphin-human comparison helps us to understand the empathy of Ghosh for endangered species of animals.

In conclusion we can see that *Gun Island* focuses on women characters who manifest the force of *shakti* in their persons. The women in the novel form a formidable brigade and influence research and social projects and are caregivers and caretakers. In this novel Ghosh has given women a space and a many-sided representation not seen hitherto in his novels.

Works Cited

Dixon, Robert. "'Travelling in the West': The Writing of Amitav Ghosh." Khair, Tabish ed. *Amitav Ghosh: A Critical Study*. Delhi: Permanent Black, 2005. 9-35.

Ghosh, Amitav. *Gun Island.* Delhi: Penguin, 2019.

_____. *Sea of Poppies*. London: Viking, 2008.

_____. *The Circle of Reason*. Delhi: Roli Books, 1986

_____. *The Hungry Tide* Delhi: Ravi Dayal, 2004.

_____. *The Shadow Lines*. Delhi: Ravi Dayal, 1988.

Ions, Veronica. Indian Mythology. London: Newnes, 1983.

Joshi, Rita. Review of *Gun Island. World Literature Today*. Vol. 93, no. 4, Autumn 2019. P. 98.

Mukerji, Sarvajit. "Against the Tide: Reading *The Hungry Tide*." R.K. Dhawan, ed. *The Novels of Amitav Ghosh*. Delhi: Prestige, 2010.

Globalization, A New Shoot with Old Root: A Study of Amitav Ghosh's *In an Antique Land* and Qurratulain Hyder's *River of Fire*

MANJUNATH G. HEGDE
SDM College, Honnavar
M.G. HEGDE
Dr. A.V. Baliga College, Kumta

Globalization is a concept usually associated with trade and economy. It is aimed at freeing the market economy by doing away with all the barriers in trades among nations. Popularly known as LPG phenomena, liberalization, privatization and globalization were initiated in the Indian economy in the 1990s consequent upon the conditions laid by the international banks to fund reform measures in Indian economy. The New Economic Policy (NEP) of the government of India has been criticized as a move towards Europeanization. The introduction of NEP coincided with the emergence of postmodern phase in the cultural life of the country. Arguably the latter is an offshoot of the former.

The social, religious and cultural life of the people was largely influenced by the LPG phenomena. The villages were exposed to the onslaught of urbanization. The metropolitan malls and industries encroached upon the conventional transactions and home industries in rural sector. Talent, skills, beliefs, language and literature were also greatly influenced. The mass culture devoured individuality. So a subtle antagonism started against this current trend.

Though economic globalization was an entirely new phenomenon of the 1990s, transaction with the outside world was not altogether a novel concept in the Indian continent. Since the Vedic period, the Indians were taught how to have the global thought. The Rig Veda preached 'Aano Bhadro Kritavo Yantu Vishwataha,' i.e., to welcome the good thoughts from every corner of the world. Thus 'thinking globally and acting locally' is ingrained in the Indians. The history of India is replete with instances of border crossings and embracing the alien elements in its cultural fabric. Historical narratives—historical novels in particular—have exploited the cultural transactions to dramatize a vision of life encapsulated in the Vedic hymn cited above. This paper is an attempt to read two Indian historical novels viz. *In an Antique Land* and *River of Fire* as responses to the process of globalization at work in the past.

Amitav Ghosh in his historical novel *In an Antique Land* has explored the overseas contact of India with Egypt. A number of traders from Egypt came to India and some of them even settled here. Not only the goods and money exchanged the hands but also their culture. Ben Yiju was a Jew trader who would marry a girl from Tulunad in Mangaluru and he would also keep a treat in a slave from the same region.

The year 1148 witnessed a number of political upheavals in the Middle East as the European armies entered the region; the kings of Germany and France in alliance made attempt to capture Damascus but in vain. In spite of all these political developments in his country and the neighboring states, Ben Yiju's letter spends no time on such things. The letter speaks more about business and a little on personal things. Yet, despite all the merchandise it speaks of, Ghosh says that the letter's spirit is anything but mercenary.

Amitav Ghosh, a social anthropologist, is a keen researcher. He has dealt with the themes of historical and cultural displacement and alienation of persons in the book. His visits to different continental countries and his interactions with multi-cultured people would have an interface with his historical investigation.

There is an attempt to understand the past through the present and vice versa. The writer is imaginative in deciphering the historical clues that he comes across in his studies. The academic journey, the studies that the writer undertakes, will lead to the speculative voyage and the interactions among the people in the past. By doing so he has reinterpreted history. Thus he shows that history is not static but growing with the times.

The writer, travelling in another country, actually discovers and after that continues the same clinging to his imagination. So the world of illusion that he creates in the processes as a myth happens to be the offshoot of contemporary history. It is also an attempt to assert his presence in the foreign land that he feels shrinking and dwindling away due to the present circumstances.

Ben Yiju began his journey towards Aden and India with a four-hundred-mile voyage on the river, Nile. Since the journey on that route was sailing against the current, it could have taken eighteen long days. Ben Yiju took this difficult direction though the same length of journey in other direction would take just eight days. He would pass through a place called Qus during the twelfth century; the same is now a modest district town a little north of Luxor. The author while quoting from Ibn Jubair, an Andulasian Arab traveller, said that it was admirably cosmopolitan with many Yemeni, Ethiopian and Italian merchants passing through it. Jubair once tried to count the caravans passing through that place. He noted that much of the cargo consisted of goods from India. There were loads of pepper: "The loads of pepper, in particular, were so many as to seem to our fancies to equal the dust in quantity." (175)

In his exploration of the relationship between India and Egypt in the distant past, the novelist sheds light on the nature of ancient civilization in the two countries. He has also checked the present state of these contacts. He came to know about this from a few people there. Sabry was one such person who was well read in such matters and gave him information. The author's love for cows was looked with amazement by the people there. His treatment of cows was even criticized. But his personality won the heart of many people there. The past friendliness between the people of the two countries had also come to his aid on some occasions. When Sabry told a woman about the author that he often went down to the fields to take picture of cows, she looked at him as her mouth fell open in amazement. The mother also insisted that the author should consider himself one of their family members. Quoting her son, Sabry, she said, "Sabry so much likes to talk to you—why, just the other day he said to me, the people of Egypt and India have been like brothers for centuries." (186)

The author in his research on the relationship between India and Egypt in the past found that there was a trade link between the two countries. A trader named Ben Yiju had left Aden and arrived in India as early as 1130 or 1131. Ben Yiju later married a slave girl named Ashu. The marriage led to Ashu's manumission. Ben Yiju must have heard about the Middle East, India that it was place notable for the ease of its sexual relations. Here the writer has opposed such generalization about Indian image. India was not as Ben Yiju thought about it. If Ben Yiju had read the works of his contemporary, Sharif al-Idrisi, he would have known facts about the then Indian situation. Sharif al-Idrisi was quoted: 'In India concubinage is permitted between everyone, so long as it is not with married woman.'

Thus India was both a receiver and a giver as far as material wealth, culture and spirituality were concerned. Though pattern of relationship among nations including India has changed from past to present, the tenor of its cosmopolitan attitudes has remained.

Qurratulain Hyder, in her novel, *River of Fire* argues for a culture that is inclusive. The novel insists that religion is irrelevant when it comes to defining of Indian Identity. She uses mythology to confront the historical facts. India has a history of thousands of years. The British came over here, colonized the country and spoiled the Hindu-Muslim amity. The difference is seen only between pre-colonial and post-colonial India after the entry of British. There was perfect coordination and co-operation among the different religious groups in ancient India. She explains her point of view through the interweaving parables, legends, dreams, diaries, and letters. Hyder questions the claim of the British Empire that it was instrumental in bringing the people together into one Nation. In fact the British divided nation and the goodwill that existed before among different communities began to wane with the entry of British.

India was already rich with religions, faiths, culture and philosophy before Jainism and Buddhism were introduced here. The philosophy which advised the renunciation of worldly life was already there. The new faiths and religions were just the extensions. Gautama said this to the prince who would come to the temple to spend the night, "One came across sophists and logisticians and atheists, former kings and princes, roving by the light of the moon as wandering philosophers. The prince of Kapilavastu had also followed this tradition by giving up the world. He had added yet another philosophy to this vast kingdom of thought, where sixty-two systems already flourished." (8)

The Indians, Greeks, Arabs, Iranians and Romans were known as civilians well in advance before the Christians. There were cultural, economic exchanges among these nationals. Later these countries were colonized by Europeans. A qazi of Tolado said, "the Indian, Greeks, Romans, Arabs and Iranians had cultivated knowledge while the people of northern Europe were uncouth barbarians. A time may soon come when those barbarians will rule the world." (58)

There was a cordial relationship between India and Iran. Many names belonging to India had been given by Iranians. Iranians were great name givers. Punj-ab means five rivers and the land of five rivers was called Punjab. The Iranians also referred to the inhabitants of Hind as Hindu and the country where Hindus were residing was called Hindustan. In Persian language, Hindu means black.

There was industrial revolution in Europe during the 19th century. It is generally said that India was industrialized by the British. After sixteenth century, Europeans went overseas in large numbers. They colonized the countries of the New World. These countries offered many opportunities to be rich. They found the Eastern countries more convenient as they were backward and politically in a shambles. It is claimed in the novel that India became a rich industrialized country when the British came here. It was exporting her textiles and luxury goods to Europe. The foreign trade was showing the downward trend due to political troubles at home and also in Iran and Turkey. A journalist said to Cyril Ashley, "We have already made short shrift of the Frogs and the chaps from the Low Countries. After the decline of the Mughals' central authority everybody in India wants to capture power at Delhi. We have almost succeeded." (106)

The rift among the Indians helped the British to make huge profit in India. Bengal had become a big market for the British traders. The British officials like Clive and Hastings facilitated the British to make profit easily in India. The Marwaris worked as middlemen for the English. Peter Jackson, a businessman, who wanted Cyril Ashley to become partner in India, told him about Indians, "They are terribly disunited. Many have become our allies. There are natives who will befriend us and turn against their own people if they find some personal profit in it." (106)

The Indian composite culture is remarkable. There were cultural exchanges between Hindu and Muslim communities over the years. Sultan-Alam Vajid Ali Shah was deposed of his throne and sent to Calcutta. On his way to Calcutta, he stopped over in Banaras and gave a large sum of money to his host, Maharaja Ishari Parsadnarain Singh. He gave this amount with the specific purpose of setting up a trust for Shehnai players to play in the main temple of kasha every morning. The Muslims were traditional Shehnai players in the Hindu temples, who had been appointed by the priests of the temples. These Shehnai players had to play their wind instrument at the temple in the morning. The playing of Shehnai was a ritual for 'waking up' the deities. Sultan-i-Alam Vajid Ali Shah's gesture of donating for the trust was a sign of the composite culture prevalent in India hundreds of years ago. "It was the parting gesture of a monarch whose predecessors had created an exquisite composite culture during the 166 years of their reign over this land." (209)

The novel has delineated the characters of different generations since the time of the heydays of Buddhism to the period of post-independence. Hyder has shown that the Indians have proved their cosmopolitan outlook over the years as the values like tolerance, broadmindedness, receiving of goodness from other races are in the very blood of Indians.

The spirit underlying the concept of globalization is not new for Indians. The sheer materialistic application of globalization has harmed the nations all over the world as it has badly affected the society, the culture and the beliefs of these countries. Globalization has to be applied in the right spirit. Other countries have to learn from the history of India.

Works Cited

Dhar, T.N., *History Fiction Interface*, New Delhi: Prestige, 1999.

Ghosh, Amitav, *In an Antique Land*, New Delhi: Ravi Dayal Publishers, 1992.

Hyder, Qurratulain, *River of Fire*, New Delhi: New Directions, 1959.

Nandy, Ashish, 'History's Forgotten Doubles,' *History and Theory*, Vol. 34, No. 2, May 1995.

Padma, V., *Fiction as Window*, Hyderabad: Orient BlackSwan, 2009.

White, Hayden, *Interpretation in History, New Literary History*, Vol. 4, No. 2, On *Interpretation: I* (Winter 1973)

Narrating the Female: Reading Gender in the Short Stories of Qurratulain Hyder

SHABINA FATIMA
Res. Sch., Dr. Bhimrao Ambedkar University, Agra

> I have chosen to no longer be apologetic for my femaleness and my feminity. And I want to be respected in all of my femaleness because I deserve to be.
>
> Chimamanda Ngozi Adichi, *We Should be All Feminists*

Females have always been trapped in the patriarchal society and discriminated against. Therefore, the female narrates her stories of life in a different way. The French feminists have established that there is a direct relation between the language that women use and the identity that they carry. The language of the male and the female is different. The language of the man displays dominance while the language of the female is kind towards man. When a female narrates her experiences, her stories are different because her language and her experiences are different. The French feminist Helen Cixous emphasized the significance of ecriture feminism. By ecriture she means that the female has to write her experiences to let the world know the experiences that women undergo. Unless she acquires the language to tell her story, the woman would not be free from the male domination. Thus, the French feminists presented a different idea to fight against the patriarchy.

This paper explores the female experience in Qurratulain Hyder's short stories through the narrative technique and language. Qurratulain Hyder in her writings has given voice to the unknown experiences of the female sufferings and miseries in the Indian situation. She has explored the complex cultural traditions and practices which helped the male to control the female. In her novels and short stories, she narrates the female experiences, especially the female in the context of Awadhi culture. This paper takes up a few stories to argue that Qurratulain Hyder has portrayed sensitively and effectively the female life of sorrows and sufferings in dominant patriarchal system. In "Honour," the protagonist Shamshad Begum suffers just because she is a female. When she was young, her property was controlled by her male cousin who does not let her use the resources. In spite of inheriting a lot of property, she has to work as a family servant. As if this is not enough, when she is old, she is taken to Bombay by another female relative and is employed to look after the home of a lady who is in flesh trade. She moves from one place to another but her problems never come to an end because of the patriarchal system.

Hyder was experimental in every piece of her writing. History appears to be a source of great sorrow and longing. "The Exiles" narrates the painful consequences of partition, feeling of exodus and exile, struggle of the human mind, cultural and moral degradation of higher society, hollowness of socio-political values, issues of class difference, aspirations for better life, tyranny of time, feeling of colour and creed, religion and nationality.

The story may be read on several grounds: a love story full of disturbances; the condition of women; a study of Indian culture and life style. The love affair between Kamal Kumari and Dr. Aftab Rai ends because of social bigotries. Being an educated and modern lady, she is clear in all her affairs; it is Aftab who ran away because he did not know "the meaningfulness of existence" (27). When Aftab left for London, Kamal had to get married to Jagan Nath Jain, ICS. She adjusts herself in the situation. As wife of an ICS officer, she engages herself in social activities like party, club, debates. On one occasion, she faces a number of silly questions: "She was simply attired, almost like a man. No jewellery. No nothing not even bangles. Bodded hair, plain georgette sari, sleeveless blouse. And no nose flower adorned her right nostril" (26).

When Aftab comes to know about Kamal's marriage from Mahipal, he immediately says: "the female tribe is an abominable tribe" (29). Contrary to this, Kamal cannot forget him and feels destroyed and wishes to die. Basically it is a reflection on female emotions and aspirations of having the right to expect something more from life than she has got and how she is controlled and manipulated. Hyder through Kamal Kumari demands a niche which is equal to man in the society. Kamal is a new woman who instead of security, comfort and respectability wants her emotional and spiritual needs to be recognized. So much is conveyed through these words: "Do you happen to know what kind of exile I am? I have been banished to live in the cocktail circuit" (51). Anees Jung voices the same concerns many years later. "My reality no longer has one face. I have stepped out of an enclosed reality into one that is larger, more diverse, and mobile. . . . I continue to live out an experience for which I have yet to find a name" (18).

Kishwari too suffers a lot due to gender bias. Born in a Zamindar family, she was an educated and modern girl who knew the latest fashion, a "forward-looking young woman . . . fond of reading" (37). She was promised to get married to Aizaz Mian but that did not happen as she was not interested in getting married to him. She plans to refuse him at the time of Nikah if she was forced to get married. She was engaged to Capt. Asghar; the proposal brings for her the opportunity to get higher education. She was sent to Lucknow where she became an activist and joined the Muslim league. She was seen everywhere: "Badminton tournaments, Debates, Activities of the Muslim Student Federation."

The story is set in the turbulent times of Indian freedom struggle and partition, which shattered the life of all Indians. Kishwari was one of those who decided to stay on in India even when all her brothers and relatives except her father migrated to Pakistan.

Her agricultural lands were taken up by tenant farmers and Asghar Abbas could not send her money which resulted in financial crisis. She tried to get a job but could not get any because it was presumed that "She was staying back because of some personal problem. The moment you get a chance, you'll also migrate" (46). She then tries for a scholarship and gets a stipend from British Council. On her way to England, she gets the news of her father's death. Upon hearing this news, she remains numb and is not able to express her grief through tears. She decides to go to the cathedral where "once she saw a pale Hungarian girl who sat there motionless, rosary in her hand, lost in deep prayer" (52). She paints a portrait and entitles it 'Escape from Freedom." She decided to make some more portraits of "the exiles, faces of despair and hope" (52). Kishwari feels that there are certain feelings which cannot be expressed through words or colour.

With the social and cultural changes in the post-independence India, she finds herself the crossroads. The consciousness of a changed time on one hand and the socio-cultural modes and values that has given her a defined role towards herself on the other hand, lead to fragmentation of the very psyche of Kishwari. The story ends with a hope: "Our exile will be over, we have before us today's dawn, the future that the new creation of the entire world." The line is suggestive of the 'becoming woman space of intersubjectivity,' a space where the world is constructed on the grounds of reducing binary opposition (man/ woman, Hindu/ Muslim, colonizer/ colonized) which should be opposed relinquished and eventually made immaterial" (Orlando 6-7).

Hyder's "The Sound of Falling Leaves" is a truthful portrayal of the plight of women in the society and their strenuous struggle to be recognized as a human being in male-dominated society. Life for the deserted Tanveer Fatima offers no choice except endless suffering. Like other women, she yearns for happiness, pleasure and a life free from all shackles and hindrances. She has memories of only bickerings, beatings, crises of depression, humiliation and frustration.

Tanveer Fatima belongs to Meerut, a small city in Uttar Pradesh. She grew up in a Zamindar family where Purdah was strictly followed and girls were kept secluded even from their cousins. Being the only daughter of her family, she was darling of her parents and got education at Aligarh and Delhi. In Delhi, she met Major Kushwaqt Singh who was a Chauhan Rajpoot. Gradually their meetings turned into a love affair.

The story ruthlessly unmasks the dual standards of morality in society in respect of man-woman relationship; the passive submissive role of a woman in man-woman relationship and the vindictive attitude of a woman in prolonging the suffering and ignoring of another woman by a male. Tanveer had this experience when she went with Kushwaqt on a trip to Ooty. Kushwaqt and she had a fight and he "hit me till my face was bloodied and my arms and legs were left with dark bruises" (73). The reason was his affair with an Indian Christian girl. Later, he proposed to her but she refused. In the later part of the story, Tanveer becomes a mistress of Faruq. She was forced to leave for Pakistan by Faruq who promised to meet her later. In the early years, Faruq visited her five-six times in a year but later on his visits became infrequent. She was left with no other choice but to work as a teacher. Then she got married to Viquar Hussain Khan, an aged already married man because "Marriage provides a roof over girl's head."(81)

Hyder's heroines pass through a transitional phase where they break traditional norms and take a new path but they fumble and turn back in anguish. Hyder's heroines are representative of the so-called emancipated educated Indian women in post-independence India. She has also shown the trauma of the partition on families, personal relationships and the females in particular. Hyder has given them the courage to break the societal mould yet somewhere or the other the innate timidity of the female either makes her compromise with the circumstances. Hyder has created a new type of female protagonist who tries to do things in a different manner yet ends up confused, bewildered and hopeless at times. What the writer is trying to display is that the woman has to make choice. The narration is a mixed bag of contradictions; we have the females swinging between hope and hopelessness, love and hatred, freedom and repulsion. The trauma especially of the Muslim women is depicted with great authenticity by Qurratulain Hyder in all her writings and especially the three stories discussed in this paper. Today in the 21st century when we are debating on issues such as 'Triple Talak,' 'Me Too' and the right of women to control their destiny, it is pertinent to see that Hyder displayed a boldness of approach so many years back but was curtailed by the social norms prevalent at that time that may have forced her heroines to fall back on solutions that would toe the social criteria. If these stories were written in the present scenario, their ending might have been different and the narratives stronger as the present-day female is much more independent than her older counterpart. Yet we have to admire Hyder's courage in showing women who are not afraid to make choices driven by the heart whatever the consequences may be and that is where Hyder succeeds as a writer. Today many voices have emerged that strive to give the female voice through their narrative even though they too feel thwarted at times. One such voice is that of Anees Jung who in her *Unveiling India* raises the literary consciousness of her reader regarding the position of women and their desire and need to speak and be heard. Anees Jung says: "Not long ago a woman who spoke about herself was considered a loose woman. To voice a pain, to divulge a secret, was considered sacrilege, a breach of family trust. Today, voices are raised without fear, and are heard outside the walls of homes that once kept a woman protected, also isolated. Some of the women who speak here have stepped out. Others who have not, are beginning to be aware, eager to find expression. But let them speak for themselves." (109)

I end this paper with lines from the poem "Khabees" by Iqra Khilji that has gone quite viral these days in the social media and states that the female today is speaking out boldly and stridently, conveying to the males in general that enough is enough:

> Nizaam-e-pidari se baghwat
> Hai tehreek meri,
> Kamzor-o-Kamzarf nahi hai ye taiweez meri
> Mai tumhare wazaarat khano
> Ka rukh bhi kar chuki hoo
> Ab ye khayal chod do ki
> Aaraaish hai takleeq meri.

The translation of this poem is:

> My mutiny is against this patriarchy
> And my schemes are neither weak or credulous
> I have made my way to the house of
> Power from where you oppress me
> It is time that you know that my creation,
> Was not the ornamentation of your world.

Works Cited

Chatterjee, Partha and Pradeep Jeganathan. *Communication Gender and Silence.* Delhi: Permanent Black, 2002.

Cixous, Helen. "The Laugh of the Medusa," trans. Keith Cohen and Paula Cohen, *Signs*: 875-93. 1976.

Hyder, Qurratulain. *The Sound of Falling Leaves.* Vol. 1, Delhi: Sahitya Akademi, 2014, pp. 18-121.

Jung, Anees. *Unveiling India: A Woman's Journey*. Penguin. 2000.

Oikkonen, Venla. "Narrative Analysis as a Feminist Method: The Case of Genetic Ancestry Test," *European Journal of Women's Studies,* 20: 3, 2013. pp. 295-308. http:/ejw.sagepub.com/content/20/3/295.

Orlando, Valerie. *Nomadic Voices of Exile*: *Feminine Identity in Francophone Literature of the Maghreb.* Ohio: Ohio U.P., 1999.

Swain, S.P. *The Feminine Voice in Indian Fiction,* New Delhi, Asia Book Club, 2005.

Raja Rao's *Kanthapura* and R.K. Narayan's *The Guide*: A Comparative Study

KONGARI SHYAM SUNDAR
CVR College of Engineering, Hyderabad
SRIDHAR MADDI
Anurag University, Hyderabad

Comparative study is a literary discipline. Etymologically, comparative literature means any literary work that compares the literary work of another writer of the same or another nation. It is a literary study across cultural, national and regional barriers. It looks at differences and affinities in different literatures. While world literature, according to Goethe, is a body of valuable works, comparative literature is a method of investigation mainly concerned with relationships, resemblances and differences. There is further attempt on the part of comparative literature to discover unity and diversity in a multilingual, multinational and multi-regional culture.

Raja Rao's *Kanthapura* was published in 1938 and R.K. Narayan's *The Guide* in 1958. While *Kanthapura* is cast in the mythical mode, *The Guide* follows the mode and technique of a typical western novel. *Kanthapura* is seen as *Harikatha* (stories of Lord Vishnu) presenting the *sthalapurana* (the legend of locality) of the village Kanthapura, an imaginary town. Following the mythical mode, the religion is presented as a series of transactions in which human beings participate. The characters in the novel are associated with Godlike persons. There is a predetermined quality, stability and fixity to the characters and there are no multiple points of view; the perspective is single and controlled. This is especially true in case of the protagonist, Murthy.

However, *The Guide* has both 'flat' and 'round' characters, the terms used by E.M. Forster in his *Aspects of the Novel*. Forster cites Mrs. Micawber in Charles Dickens' *David Copperfield* as an example of a 'flat' character. Elizabeth in Jane Austen's *Pride and Prejudice* and Henchard in Thomas Hardy's *The Mayor of Casterbridge* are good examples of a 'round' character. In *The Guide*, Macro and Raju's mother are flat characters whereas Raju and Rosie are round characters. Initially, Rosie is presented as a beautiful woman interested in developing her artistic skill and finding fulfillment. By the middle of the novel, however, when Raju is taken away by the police, she has grown into a far more mature woman leading a life of vitality.

As for Raju, the protagonist, it is perhaps not very accurate to say that he radically changes in the course of the novel. His transformation from a tourist guide to a spiritual guide and from a criminal to a saint figure is caused by the circumstances. While narrating his past to Velan, Raju complains: "It is written on the brow of some that they shall not be left alone. I am on search. Even the prison is a kind of supervisor and personal secretary to the superintendent." But there is an internal struggle at least with regard to his role of a saint. This struggle indicates a change of character, especially when he examines his motives for undertaking a fast.

There is another major difference in the two novels when we look at their protagonists. In a typical British or American novel, the protagonist is not a person of high estate, as the protagonists in classical and Shakespearian tragedies were. Tom Jones, Oliver Twist, Rebecca Sharp, Tess, Easter Prynne—none of these main characters possessed heroic qualities in the beginning. But they achieve significance and even nobility in the course of the novel. It is in this sense that the novel has been called truly democratic in form.

In Narayan's *The Guide*, the protagonist is an ordinary man. He blunders through life and acts from motives which are not noble in nature. In Raja Rao's *Kanthapura,* on the other hand, Murthy is conceived as extraordinary from the very beginning. The difference in the conception of characters leads to a difference in the way the characters act. In *The Guide*, the circumstances determine action. Coming of the railway in Malgudi turns Raju into a guide. Velan, the unquestioning devout believer in the new Swami, is responsible for creating a community of followers and worshippers around Raju. On the contrary, Murthy in *Kanthapura* is never forced into any action because of circumstances. For example, the incident of fasting in the two novels. While fasting is almost forced upon Raju as a result of tragi-comic misunderstanding, the fasting by Murthy is a conscious decision undertaken as a means of purifying himself and setting an example of leadership.

As observed earlier, *Kanthapura* reveals a single unified point of view and lacks multiple perspectives. The narrative mode makes it possible. In *The Guide*, there is a double narrative mode. One part of the novel is in autobiographical mode and is narrated in the first person by Raju. The other part is in the omniscient mode. This technique ensures the double perspective. Events are seen both through Raju's eyes as well as through more objective eyes of the author. Thus, present and past alternate showing that Raju's present is inexorably rooted in his past.

Use of double perspective in *The Guide* results in the ambivalence of our attitude to the protagonist. The narrative technique ensures that our attitude to Raju does not stabilize. The fifth chapter, narrated in the past, closes with the seduction of Rosie by Raju. This evokes a negative disapproving response from us. When the novel resumes the narration in the present, it contains the commitment to the past and that surely evokes a different kind of response from us. In contrast, the narrative technique in *Kanthapura* controls and organizes our responses in a stable and unified way, leaving no room for any ironic perspective.

Kanthapura has caste dominant political ideology of the times namely the ideology of nationalism. Is it possible to make a similar political reading of *The Guide*? The impact of western literature on Narayan is obvious from the novel which was written in different narrative modes and techniques. The powerful presence of comic irony is another important link that ties Narayan to the British novelists. But there are no assertions of national identity or the glory and greatness of Indian past and present. There is no place for that kind of thing in *The Guide*. Since it is a post-independence novel written in 1958, it presents the post-independence India rather than reawakening of a village or people of a nation in colonized nation.

Works Cited

Forster E. M. Forster. *Aspects of the Novel*. New York: Rosetta, 2002.

Iyengar, K.R. Srinivasa. *Indian writing in English*. 1962; New Delhi: 1983. 358-411.

Mukerjee, Meenakshi. *The Twice-Born Fiction. Themes and Techniques of the Indian Novel in English*. New Delhi: Heinemann, 1971.

Naik, M.K. *A History of Indian English Literature*, New Delhi: Sahitya Akademi, 1982.

Narayan, R.K. *The Guide*. 1958; Mysore: Indian Thought Publications, 1963.

Rao, Raja. *Kanthapura*. 1938; Delhi: Oxford University Press, 2003.

Trivedi, Harish. "Gandhian Nationalism: Kanthapura," *Literature of Nation: British and India 1800-1900*, ed. Richard Allen and Harish Trivedi. London: Routledge, 2000. 107-20

Walsh, William. *R.K. Narayan: A Critical Appreciation*. London Heinemann, 1982.

Jatin Bala:
The Politics of Being a Dalit in Bengal

BRATI BISWAS
Dyal Singh Evening College, University of Delhi

Bengal is not known either for caste uprisings or for caste-based politics. Therefore, it is concluded that caste is not a very visible entity in the social, political and cultural fabric of Bengal. On the other hand, the Dalits, who form a sizeable portion of Bengal's population,[1] affirm that they have been victims of casteist discrimination for ages and continue to suffer innumerable indignities on account of their caste. Daipayan Halder's article "Casteless, Classless, Truthless," brings to the fore the question of caste oppression in Bengal and the silence around this topic: "Most of those familiar with Kolkata--and the *bhadralok* ethos it celebrates--will tell you that in this city, atrocities based on caste bias are but stray incidents. . . . On the surface, yes, it may be different in Bengal. . . . Urban Bengal has always had 'a tradition of unorthodoxy.' . . . But that has not put a stop to caste crimes here. It's another matter that they mostly go unreported . . . the government of the proletariat has been guilty not only of criminal negligence to the Dalit cause, but of atrocities against them as well."[2]

Daipayan Haldar reports that in rural Bengal, Dalit families are marginalized and forced to live a life of shame and suffering. In November 2004, students in a primary school in Birbhanpur village in West Bengal's Bankura district refused to accept midday meals because the cook was an untouchable *baghdi* woman. A similar incident took place in Purulia district's Dumuradi village around the same time. "After the mid-day meal incident the *Anandabazar Patrika* ran a series on the plight of Dalits in Bengal villages. . . . In village after village, the survey finds that Dalit families are marginalized, Dalit children are made to occupy separate seats in schools and are denied access to libraries and other facilities" (Haldar). This proves that in matters of casteism, Bengal is no different from the rest of India. The pervasive caste bias in urban and rural Bengal is the oft-iterated theme of Dalit writings emanating from there. Dalit writers like Jatin Bala contend on the urgent need to highlight and expose caste-based discrimination and biases in every sphere--from society and politics to the writing of literature and history.

Jatin Bala was born in 1949 in Jessore in a peasant family belonging to the Namasudra caste. He spent his youth in different refugee camps and did various jobs to sustain himself. He worked as a Block youth officer of the state government and this brought him in close contact with the poor Dalit villagers of West Bengal and they form the core of his narratives. His stories are about caste relations in Bengal and Dalit self-awakening within the context of the Dalit movement at large.

Bala explores the complex nuances of the Dalit individual's relationship with his community through the Dalit protagonists of his stories. He explores the issue of Dalit unity and solidarity vis-à-vis Brahminic hegemony and power. The fragile nature of Dalit unity and the successful coming together of the Brahmans in his stories reflect the power wielded by the combination of caste and class in the case of the Brahmans. The Brahman's power emanates from their social and economic dominance over the Namasudra peasants. The Brahmans use their power and cunning to silence the Dalits. The new awakened Dalit individual critiques both the Dalit and Brahman communities. This self offers a ray of hope for Dalit liberation.

In "Payer Talar Mati" (The Soil Under the Feet)[3] he represents a vocal and conscious Dalit rebel in the figure of Haladhar Haldar.

Haladhar is a Namasudra peasant and a good mason. He represents him as a tall, broad shouldered, simple, uncomplicated and open natured man. Haladhar antagonizes the Brahmans of the village when he critiques their ritual of offering 'tarpan' or water to their ancestors while bathing. The Brahman, Gopal Chakraborty, sees Haladhar copying him and asks him since when did the Dalit Namasudra begin to adopt Brahmanical ways. Haladhar replies that he was giving water to his fields and not to his ancestors. Chakraborty sarcastically questions that was the water taking a heavenly route to reach his fields. Haladhar replies that it is taking the same route taken by their water to reach their ancestors. The Brahmans do not like Haladhar's sarcastic reference to their practice and decide to teach the insubordinate Dalit a lesson. They wonder at his audacity to criticize or question their religious and ritualistic practices. The predominant feeling was that the lower castes were fast becoming insubordinate and if they were not controlled well in time they would not obey the Brahmins. The Brahmins of the village were well placed. Haren Mukherjee the Oil mill owner, Haru Roy the rice mill proprietor, the Ration shop owner Harish Das Sharma, the Panchayat President Neel Kamal Bhattacharya and others come together to consult to teach Haladhar a lesson. They warn him to respect the Brahminical traditions touted as the tradition of the village or he would not be allowed to stay there. In other words the 'ground beneath his feet' would be snatched away by the dominant caste as punishment for mocking them. The Dalit peasant's expression of an independent mind was a threat to Brahminic hegemony and dominance.

The headman of Anandapur village was Bhabanicharan Roy who used to employ Haladhar as a mason as he was honest and a good worker. Haladhar's workmanship was admired by the people passing by. The writer subtly creates a counter image of the Dalit as an intelligent, rational human being as opposed to the dominant representation of the Dalit as dim witted, lazy and dishonest. The common perception about the Dalits is played upon by the

Brahmins of Ichapasar, Haladhar's village to poison Bhabanicharan Roy's mind against Haladhar. They steal the jewels adorning the deity in his temple and blame it on Haladhar.

Unjustly framed he was tied to a tree and beat up till he became unconscious. They burnt down his thatched house and even tried to molest his wife. They drive her out of the village with her five-day old baby and young child. The destruction of his material assets results in his self-awakening. He walks out of the village broken in body but with an indomitable spirit to survive. He questions dominant norms. He represents the Dalit individuals' potential to grow through resistance and protest. The politics of being a Dalit writer also involves the question of aesthetics which Jatin Bala takes up in "Koshti Pathor" (59).

The story "Koshti Pathor" is set in a remote village called 'Hishabi' and focuses on the life of Sebadasi a Dalit woman who is forced by circumstances to take on the responsibility of earning a living and caring for an ill husband. The narrator of the story is a Dalit writer aspiring to create a different aesthetics based on his experience of the world of his people. He does not find the popular modes of storytelling interesting and wants to experiment with realistic narration and therefore follows Sebadashi's story. Jatin Bala uses this narrative to present the Dalit writer as a theorist and seeker of a new aesthetic to present their reality.

The writer in the story hopes to find a critic who will appreciate the realistic portrayal of the suffering of the Dalits in his stories. He connects with his characters through empathy as he is one of them. His people are close to nature and life and his technique becomes his means of asserting his 'difference' from the dominant crowd. The writer says that the days of sympathy-based literature are gone and the demand is for 'empathy'. He suggests that this feeling of empathy comes from caste kinship and a shared background. The writer in the narrative writes about his own experience of saving Sanatan Biswas when he falls from the train. He thus erases the distance between himself and his subject, fact and fiction.

Bala notes that the subject matter of the writer is not failed people but fighters who know how to survive. The peasant woman Sebadasi is a fighter and has the power to inspire the writer. This is a pointed reference to dominant depiction of the Dalit as a failed individual. The Dalit writer in the story can empathize with his characters because he too is a survivor. His father used to hawk roasted peanuts in the local trains that his mother used to prepare. Bala says, "Somewhere there is a deep bond between his life and the life story he narrates and therein lies the strength of his pen" (62). The writer represents his characters as his "soul relatives," the touchstone of an authentic representation.

The writer meets Sebadasi again after a gap of a few years and cannot fathom the change in her from a demure wife to a cussing woman. He asks her about her son and she informs him that he has got a new mother. The educated son does not want to acknowledge his old, uneducated mother. She informs him: "when a woman grows old she is of no use to anybody" (64). Her face, distorted with hate, looks very ugly. The writer moves away as he realizes that she is unable to recognize him. The writer is not able to accept the tremendous change in Sebadasi. His ambivalence towards her suggests his lack of sensitivity or empathy for the Dalit woman. He remains limited by his male point of view. The process of writing is equated to the process of giving birth but it is represented as the "superior labour" because writing can destroy the "darkness" within people (65).

In "Bargkhetrer Chaturtho Bahu" (The Fourth Arm of the Circumference), Jatin Bala speaks in his own voice as a Dalit author. He states that he writes about the injustice and oppression he witnesses. The context of the story is an award ceremony organized to encourage successful farmers. Johor Sarkar, a resident of Shona village, interests the author who likes his open nature. Johor, a Namasudra, had fled East Pakistan after the riots and settled in West Bengal. He recounts his experience in the Brahman locality and says that casteism in Bengal operates subtly and terms it a "cold war" (thanda ladai) (81). The Namasudra refugees had at first taken shelter in the Brahman locality but they soon discover that members of their group begin to die mysteriously. The local people refuse to sell land to the 'lower caste for fear they would settle there permanently and grow in strength. They are forced to leave and settle in a new place which they make habitable. He asserts that in spite of the adversities, he "did not get lost or become a loser" (82). The refugees reflect a strong pioneer spirit. Johor narrates how the villagers refer to them as 'Nomo' and treat them as untouchables. He speaks about an incident where he had once saved a girl from drowning in the neighbouring 'upper caste' village and the mother of the girl purified her with holy Ganges water before taking her home. The author visits Shona village again after a gap of five years and finds that Johor has become mad after the massacre of twenty-one Dalit peasants of his village. The rational, vocal Dalit protagonist was rendered speechless by the violence.

Bala thus points to the close relation between the Dalit and his communal self. Most of Bala's stories reflect the fissures within the Dalit community and self. These ruptures hinder the formation of a homogenous Dalit unit where the various Dalit selves would seamlessly cohere. Thus, the Dalit writer fails to empathize with, his female subject, and the community fails to sympathize with and care for Johor.

NOTES

The paper is part of the author's unpublished research, "Emergent Identities: Images of Self in Bangla Dalit Literature." JNU, 2013.

1. According to 1981 census the total population of scheduled castes in West Bengal amounted to 22 percent of the whole population of the state. Qtd. Partha Chatterjee, 'Caste and Politics in West Bengal,' *Land, Caste and Politics in Indian States*, ed. Gail Omvedt, Delhi: Authors Guild, 1982, p. 90.
2. Daipaiyan Haldar, "Casteless, Classless, Truthless," *Hindustan Times*, 15 February 2005.
3. Jatin Bala, *Gandir Bandhe Bhangan*. Kolkata: Chaturtha Duniya, 2000.

The "Unfixed Self"[1]: Expulsion of Asians from Uganda and the Popular Narratives of Indian-East African Double Diaspora

JYOTI JAKHAR DAHIYA
Moti Lal Nehru Eve. College, University of Delhi

> Man is the storytelling Animal, and that in stories are his identity, his meaning, and his lifehood. (Salman Rushdie)

> All stories are fictions. (Hayden White)

The presence of the Indian Diaspora could be arguably dated back to two thousand years.[2] However, it is the diverse and vibrant Diaspora of the last two centuries, which has been extensively documented and evidently is in a complex relationship within itself and in relation to India. Broadly, the Indian Diaspora could be grouped into two ('Old' and 'New'), depending on the different political and socio-economic conditions under which it materialized.

There is a significant difference between the 'Old' and the 'New' Indian Diaspora, to borrow Vijay Mishra's classification.[3] Old Indian Diaspora refers to the migration of the Indian people in the nineteenth century, primarily as indentured labour, to the British colonies. The 1833 law of Britain abolishing slavery is seen as a triggering force in the evolution of the Old Indian Diaspora. This migration is conventionally seen as complete, involuntary and as a consequence of poor economic condition in British India. The New, on the other hand, broadly refers to the mass movement of the professionals from India to the West, 1960s onwards. As discussed in the works of Vijay Mishra, this Diaspora is voluntary, empowered, and is more connected with the homeland. The Old merges into the New with re-migrations but there is a clear distinction between the singly and doubly hyphenated diasporas. The categories could be further complicated by inflecting these with the class, regional and religious dimensions.

Narratives connect people. Narratives connect the past, the present and shape the future. The production and consumption of popular narratives reflect as much on the writer/ producer as it does on the reader/ consumer. Popular narratives involve the politics of production, consumption and the market targeted for distribution and sale. Narratives add emotional dimension and humanize the statistical data. The recollection of narratives re-invents the past to comprehend and comment on the present. The narratives can also inflect the normalized meta narratives. They can challenge the given and redirect for an evolved society. The paper studies the narratives emerging from the Indian (double) diaspora of East Africa against the popular literature of the Indian Diaspora which is produced and circulated in the literary market place.

The present paper studies the Old and now re-migrated (and re-merged into the New) Indian Diaspora of East Africa through select movies and literary narratives. It looks at the select work of the doubly hyphenated writers of Indian origin including M.G. Vassanji (Indian-Kenyan-Canadian), Yasmin Ladha (Indian-Tanzanian-Canadian, later moved to Korea and currently in Oman), Peter Nazareth (Goan Indian-Ugandan-American) and Abraham Verghese (Indian-Ethiopian-American), Ian Iqbal Rashid (Indian-Tanzanian-Canadian) to deliberate on the subsequent issues:

- The distinctiveness of the twice displaced Indian Diaspora of East Africa and the literature of Diaspora emerging from the same.

- An analysis of the literary responses to the expulsion of the Indians from Uganda which appears as a dominant reference point in the above-mentioned literature.
- The questions of identity, memory and homeland as addressed through the narratives.
- The differences within diasporas and underscoring the differences in the narratives of the singly hyphenated [New] and the doubly hyphenated [Old] Diaspora.
- How the cultural industry promotes specific variety of cultural products to 'Other' the diaspora and maintain the binary of identity between the Diasporans and the 'true' citizens in the nation state.
- How the doubly hyphenated Indian Diaspora of East Africa illustrates the potential to challenge that and celebrate transnationalism.

The Old and the New Diasporas are products of different historical conditions.[5] Though the presence of Indian diaspora in Africa predates European civilization, Old diaspora has a distinctive connotation. The Old diasporans immigrated under the British rule as indentured labourers with their homeland carried in a 'gunny sack.' They never returned home and their migration has been understood as 'complete.' Their connection with the homeland is understood to have remained symbolic and limited. The members of the New Diaspora immigrated voluntarily and as professionals. The economically and socially empowered members are in the age of "globalization and hypermobility . . . with modern means of communication" (Mishra 3). The New Diaspora is more coupled with the homeland. The two diasporas are distinct in their disposition.

The story of the Old Indian-East African Diaspora is a complex one. As recounted in most narratives (historical, literary, popular and academic) the Indians were brought to work on the rail roads and eventually settled down.[6] In the nineteenth and the twentieth century they were less than 2% of the total population but had important role in the economic and political story of the region. They were the businessmen, the doctors, the clerks, the civil servants, the lawyers and the accountants. In the multi-racial social paradigm, most Africans remained in menial jobs. The Asians provided the required middle class in the colonial setup. The society remained racially stratified. The popular narratives depict the Indians as an exploitative middle class which was neither subjected to colonial oppression nor did it participate in the nation building project.[7]

As per the dominant discourse, the Indians in East Africa stayed isolated and culturally exclusive. The Africans regarded them as exploitative and did not trust them. A short film produced by *Thames TV* captures that emotion clearly. They maintained the racial segregation. They did not marry the Africans and maintained the social distance. They remain 'a race apart' (Dimbleby). The racial arrogance of an Indian business gets reflected in his answer to the reporter about his last thirty years in Uganda,

> Very easy earning . . . Easy life . . . and people of Uganda are not bad. [Asians are successful] because the Africans they didn't know the business . . . how can they? [Because] to run the business and to run the factories, without brain nobody can do it.

This arrogance is reflective of the nature of the dominant race relations between the Asians and the Africans.

In 1972, General Idi Amin, in his "Asian farewell speech" gave the Asians ninety days to leave the country. He accused the people of Asian origin of "sabotaging Uganda's economy and encouraging corruption . . . [and claimed that] we are determined to make the ordinary Ugandan master of his own destiny. . . . Our deliberate policy is to transfer the economic control of Uganda into the hands of Ugandans, for the first time in our country's history" (http://en.m.wikipedia.org/wiki/Expulsion_of_Asians_from_Uganda). Around eighty thousand Asians (including twenty-three thousand citizens) were made to leave Uganda. Though other East African countries did not follow the model, the Asians migrated in large numbers from the other East African countries as well (Lal 259).

The populist decision of Asian expulsion by General Idi Amin in 1972 was rejoiced by the Africans. He consolidated his position among the various conflicting African tribes by targeting the common enemy. One of the Africans when asked about the expulsion, in the abovementioned film, responds, "It's good. It's good for them to go. . . . They have sucked us enough." The response seems representative of the larger sentiment. Many welcomed the fact that the Asians were given limited time so they may not redirect resources and take away the money. Most showed no empathy for the predicament of the Asians. One of them said, "but for people who have been living with Asians, we know how much they can panic . . . they are known as the most panicky people in the world . . . there is not cause to worry."

Most narratives highlight the colonialist strategy of the British authorities in directing the Africans against the Indians. The Asians evaluated the role of the British in the changed dynamics as divisive. They saw themselves as being exploited by the White man in this arrangement of race in social hierarchy. Describing the role of the British in fictitious country Damibia in *The General is Up*, a character rationalizes: "Wherever they went, they brought in a buffer, scapegoat middle class, usually from another part of the empire. So, when Independence came, the people would be made in a thousand ways to blame these foreign scapegoats as the real cause of continued problems facing the people."

After being in Africa for over a century, the legitimacy of their citizenship and right to live in the country of birth was put to question. In Uganda the exodus was a result of State order. In adjoining countries, the fear of the same and hostile attitude of the Black Africans resulted in mass exodus of the Indians from East Africa.

Like Uganda, in Kenya too, the dominant perception of the Indians was that of the "agents of colonial regime."[8] The majority of Indians in Kenya left for Britain in late 1960s and early 1970s as "Kenya tightened residency and employment rules and promoted Africanization." (*Ibid.*)

The doubly displaced, doubly hyphenated diasporic community responds distinctly to the idea of 'home.' The distinct history of East African-Indian Diaspora can provide a framework in conceptualizing this diaspora. Being forced to exile, the mutation in the collective consciousness and identity is distinctive. The homeland consciousness can vary in a wide spectrum from the diaspora being actively involved in the socio-political-economic situation of the homeland to associating it with multiple physical location, to viewing it as an idea to be replicated and recreated wherever the communities move. This paper studies selected popular narratives to understand how the idea of home gets manifested.

> "Who will stop him?" persisted Josephine. "India? How many millions don't die in India of starvation? And has India shown any interest in the plight of Indians being expelled from Damibia? It is only interested in pointing out to Britain that British Indians are the responsibility of Britain. Which is true enough, but the East Indians and Goans are being turned into soccer balls, to be kicked wherever the players want. (Nazareth 89)

> Why do you call me "guest"/ When here I have a home,/ When here my father lived and dies,/ My mother too, and a brother?/ Their graves lie there within this City's bounds,/ Where I myself was born,/ My children too—all three of them./ Must they and I leave this land, / Be strangers to it/ Because your skin is black and mine and theirs is brown,/ Your folk came here some scores of years ere ours?[9]

As a result of the independence of the African countries and their Africanization, Britain witnessed a large inflow of Asian Africans post 1965. In 1968, Britain came up with 'restriction act'[10] which allowed the migration of only those British citizens who had a parent or a grandparent born in Britain (Lal 259). Most of the Asian Ugandans at the time of exile had British protected passports. They had worked for the British imperial power as the desired "middle class" in the African colonies. They have been conventionally viewed by both themselves and the Africans as working on behalf of the British. Most were neither Ugandan nor British citizens but held British protected passports. In wake of the expulsion rule, most looked towards Britain as the obvious second home. Britain was forced to take in twenty-seven thousand 'refugees.' Ugandan Resettlement Board, with Sir Charles Cunningham as its Chairman, was set up to "not to overwhelm"[11] certain areas with the numbers and disperse the Asians throughout the country. There were mass protests against Asian immigration in some areas like Leicester City with the narrative of putting pressure on the social services. However, Home Secretary Robert Carr acknowledges the 'obligation' to take them in. Some reports suggest that with passage of time, the Asians felt well settled. In 1997, businessman Manubhai Madhvani said, "We came here 25 years ago full of anxiety to an unknown land. The British people extended a welcoming hand enabling us to make this country our home. Very few people tend to say thank you. We intend to be different." (www.theyworkforyou.com/lords/?id=2012-12-06a.802.0)

Years later, on 6 December 2012, the house of Lords debated (moved by Lord Popat) and made a "note of the contribution made by the Ugandan Asian community in the United Kingdom on the occasion of the 40th anniversary of their expulsion from Uganda."

Asian Africans did not find much support from the Indian government. In 1954, the Prime minister Jawaharlal Nehru had preferred a better relationship with the host countries rather than with the diasporans. The newly independent India was still recovering from the horrors of Partition, the dismal economic condition and the project of nation building. Situation in India did not make it a desired country to go back to. In 1972, post expulsion order, the Prime minister Indira Gandhi was quick to cut diplomatic ties with Uganda but the country was busy healing from a war with Pakistan and creation of Bangladesh. The politically unstable environment in the region further deterred the exiled Indians to consider India as a desired option to migrate to. Most contemporary Asian East Africans had been in East Africa for more than a century and India was not viewed as a homeland by this generation.

A large number of Ismaili Indians migrated to Canada. Most of them were Ugandan citizens and Britain was not obligated to take them in. The role of the Ismaili spiritual leader, Aga Khan IV, needs to be underscored. His personal friendship with the Canadian Prime minister, Pierre Trudeau, became contributory in the safe immigration of over 7000 Ugandan Asians to Canada. Canada, which "did not own the debt of hospitality"[12] willingly took anybody. In a CBC radio program "Identities" (1979), prominent families narrate the horror of leaving Kampala and a non-hostile reception in Canada.

In Uganda, as per Anthony Hughes, editor of the magazine *Africa*, it became a popular decision and consolidated the dictator's mass base. He used the Asians as "the scapegoats." As per his analysis, General Idi Amin was "not a man who has had any intellectual training . . . could not deal with the complexities of the political affairs and the diplomatic affairs" (*Ibid.*). The international condemnation of the act did not change the ground reality.

The question of race and identity had surfaced emphatically in postcolonial East Africa. The highly stratified society with very limited intermingling of the European, Asian and indigenous African races had further weakened the race relations. This resulted in the fleeing of Asians from adjoining countries like Kenya and Tanzania as well.

M.G. Vassanji responds to a question on homeland in one of the interviews: "If you do not belong to one world completely, then you can empathize with many worlds" but, "When you belong to two worlds, you are always losing because worlds are dynamic."[13] Many theorists have deliberated and verbalized this dynamic relationship between the Diasporans and the idea of home.

William Safran in his most-quoted definition of Diaspora sees homeland as a geographical entity and claims that members of Diaspora "regard their ancestral homeland as their true, ideal home and as the place to which they or their descendants would (or should) eventually return—when conditions are appropriate." Safran's definition essentializes the Diasporic identity, views the connect with the homeland as a desire to physically return. However, the Indian-East African Diasporic people, when faced with that tough choice to leave, moved towards the West and not to India.

This historical development reflects on the complex relationships the Diasporans have, especially the twice displaced East African Indians, with their "ancestral homeland." The emotional and economic ramifications of the forceful expulsion find representation in the popular literature and motion pictures. Two movies directed by Mira Nair, *Mississippi Masala* (1992) and *My Own Country* (1998), discuss the complex relation of the twice displaced Diasporans to (the idea of) home.

Mississippi Masala recounts the journey of a third generation Indian-Ugandan family, post exodus. Jay, a wealthy Indian-Ugandan is made to leave Kampala with just the essentials. The family feels betrayed and all three characters (Jay, Kinni and their young daughter Mina) express fear and grief on the screen. The movie opens with Jay asking his African friend, "But where should I go? . . . this is my home." The friend responds: "Africa is for Africans. Black Africans." Years later Jai recounts how it was not General Idi Amin but this viewpoint that pushed them and other Indians out of Uganda. It is Uganda which reserves Jai's yearning. It is Uganda which appears in Mina's dreams. Jai spends most of his life fighting for his property with the contemporary Ugandan regime. Jai is a member of the Old Indian Diaspora, "where imagination [of the (Indian) homeland] was triggered by the contents in gunny sacks: a Ganesha icon, a dog-eared copy of the *Ramayana* or the *Qura'n,* an old sari or other *deshi* outfit, a photograph of a pilgrimage, and so on" (Mishra 2005: 4). His India is fossilized and dated. The Indian attire and music find a place in their lives but the heart clearly belongs to Uganda. However, years later when Jai returns to Uganda for a court hearing, he finds that his idea of Uganda does not match with the contemporary reality. The movie ends with his resolution that "home is where the heart is."

My Own Country is based on Abraham Verghese's semi-autobiographical work. Expelled from his country in East Africa, Abraham, a doctor of Indian origin, decides to immigrate to the US. A specialist in infectious diseases, he settles in Johnson City, Tennessee. He works with the AIDS patients with a lot of empathy and compassion. His non-judgemental attitude wins him love and respect. The memoir/ movie does not focus on the sense of loss but on the emotion of benevolence. Though the movie opens with the narrator's lamentation that "when you are forced to leave a country you once called home, it changes everything. You can't appreciate the simple pleasures of life, you envy people around you who could," this is not the emotion the movie focuses upon. The sense of loss is expressed through the character of Verghese's wife, Ragini. A first-generation immigrant, Ragini, is a professional classical dancer from South India. She first loses her audience and then the joy of dancing, even in private. The unavailability of her husband, even at the time of her delivery, compounds her alienation. However, the focus of the work is on the sense of belonging doctor Abraham Verghese has to the cause of AIDS. The narrator calls Tennessee his own country. The sense of home is not associated with the country of birth but a geographical space which gave him a purpose in life. The sense of belonging is viewed beyond the established parameters of race and nation.

The personal journey of writer M.G. Vassanji highlights this complex relation between the doubly hyphenated diasporans and the idea of home. His novels are set in India, East Africa and

Canada. In an interview with Charles Foran, his passionate concern for East Africa suggests that his heart belongs to Dar es Salam and Kariakoo (an Indian neighbourhood) which he says, for him, is "a living place . . . more alive than Toronto (http://www. macleans. ca/culture/books). However, the title of the book, *And Home Was Kariakoo: A Memoir of East Africa*, suggests that it is a thing of the past. In another interview when asked about the setting of his novel *The Assassin's Song* in Gujarat, India, he says it is "the burden of tradition . . . part of my history [and I wanted to] discover myself, discover how I fitted into not only history of Africa but history of India and cultures of India" (http://www.booklounge.ca/catalog/diaspora). But when asked where home is, he says "Toronto" (The Agenda with Steve Paikin, Toronto: TV Ontario). These answers highlight the complex relationship between the 'unfixed' Diasporic community and the idea of home.

The works discussed here challenge the conventional viewpoint about homeland. The idea of homeland is dissociated with a geographical entity. The idea of belonging is problematized. The possibility of belonging to multiple cultures is explored. The conservative confines of defining 'home' and 'homeland' are pressed.

Who am I? What community/ communities could I belong to? How am I viewed? How do I wish to be viewed?—these simple questions direct towards the construction and conservation of identity both at personal and collective levels. The question of identity is one of the most pressing ones for the diasporans. As presented through most cultural products like films, advertisements, music and literature, they seem to struggle between the desire to preserve the past and assimilate with the mainstream. James Clifford describes Diasporic consciousness as "'entirely a product of cultures and histories in collision and dialogue' . . . [and an awareness of] ethical or racial difference emerges against a dominant cultural force, which challenges the diasporic subject's sense of identity" (qtd. Kalra, Kaur and Hutynuk 30). For most commercially driven narratives of New diasporic literature, identity is viewed in terms of race, ethnicity and nation. However, in narratives from the contemporary doubly hyphenated (Old diaspora merged into the new), there is a paradigm shift.

Popular narratives can be viewed as going through five stages as per Todorov's narrative theory: equilibrium, disequilibrium, acknowledgement, solving and equilibrium (http://mikedyera2 mediastudies.blogspot.com/p/todorovs-theory.html?m=1). Personal narratives, when studied in this format, reflect the stages of identity formation. A study of popular cultural products by the makers/ writers from the doubly hyphenated diaspora uncover an interesting shift in comparison to the positioning of the singly hyphenated diasporic community.

The mainstream movie *Touch of Pink* (2004) is written and directed by an East African-Indian-British writer and director Ian Iqbal Rashid. It explores the difficulties faced by a young, gay Muslim man, Alim, to come out to his single mother. Alim was born to the Ismaili Indian family in Kenya. The family later settles in Toronto from where Alim moves to London. The movie is a romantic comedy. The question of identity based on original homeland has been directly addressed in the movie at two points. Alim is asked once in the Indian store by the Pakistani shopkeeper, 'Where are you from?' Secondly, on the flight to Toronto, he is asked by a co-passenger, "Are you visiting or going back home?" In both cases, the character dismisses the question and mentions that he belongs to India, Kenya, Toronto and England. The movie refuses to look at identity strictly in terms of nation and homeland. The narrative dissociates the question of identity with territory. Shifting the emphasis, it is the religious and the queer identity that connect people from different races. The 'disequilibrium' and eventual 'equilibrium' focuses on the queer identity.

It is the 'Ismaili Shia' identity which is evoked and connects the characters in the narrative. It is the Ismaili wedding and customs and the mother's question, "you don't have the picture of the Aga Khan," that stir a sense of identity in the characters. The mother's first objection to her son's (assumed) lover is that she is 'not a Muslim' but later believes that one could be 'converted.' Mother Nuru Jahan's final acceptance of her son's queer lover, publicly, brings the eventual equilibrium (Todorov 1969) to the narrative. The movie consciously moves the vocabulary of debate to other markers of identity from that of home/ host land.

In some of the works of the twice displaced diasporans, the racial binaries disband. Yasmin Ladha, in *Lion's Granddaughter*, questions the binaries in identity formation:

> *Readerji,* is this binary inevitable? One is the colonizer, the other, the colonized. Then whoa, whoa *Readerji*. Now, please pick up speed and move! *Chapa chapa*, tout-suite (clap clap), *fatafat*, out of my text because I shy/ sly from any confinement/ circle/ missionary position. Friction/ fiction between mates facilitates ousting of hierarchical positions. I don't want to be the sturdy alphabet to set a novice at ease in Other literature—a vaccination prior to his/ her flight into the Third World. But sometimes this has to be done, then I can't help it. (Lal 131)

When asked about identity, the Canadian writer Yasmin Ladha tells the interviewer that identity is 'osmosis' (Interview with Jasleen Vohra in *Aaj Savere*, Delhi Doordarshan National, 4 years ago. http://youtube/b62oLul81gl). Though 'connected to India,' she wishes to refer to her as a writer from Canada but she celebrated the idea of giving her 'many hyphens.' This plurality is reflected in her craft. Her work *Blue Sunflower Startle* cannot be fixed to one genre. Belonging simultaneously to the genres of novel, essay and poetry, the genre is as "unfixed" as the writer's identity. The coherence of the book/ identity finds its way through apparently contradictory genres/ identity markers.

Where the Air is Sweet by Tasneem Jamal is a semi-autobiographical novel set in Uganda in the time period 1921-75. Through the complicated race relations of three generations in Uganda, it looks at the eventual expulsion of the family. The colonizer/ colonized binaries are blurred. The plight of the Indian family to restart their lives in utter chaos, post expulsion order, find expression in this emotional family saga. "Her characters straddle the permeable, ever-shifting line between homes, between overlapping identities, between longing and belonging, desire and hope" (Ayelet Tsabari, book review, Amazon.in). The shock of the inexplicable ethnic cleansing, the feeling of letting go, forms the core of the book. However, as the title suggests, the end draws towards the "sense of movement, the impulse we all have to seek a better life, to go somewhere we can authentically be more, who we are, and sometimes we do have to leave what we have known for centuries." (Jamal, interview to TVO, http://youtu.be/bBqTCpry4WM)

The works argue towards an identity consciousness which is 'nomadic.'[14] The diasporans are working towards negotiating between multiple cultures. Homi Bhabha's ideas on describing the diasporic identities as 'hybrids' with 'cultural ambivalence' finds resonance here. Mostly, the resonance of celebration of belonging to multiple cultures overrides the dismay of struggles of assimilation.

The representation of Asians in various narratives reaffirm that Asians in East Africa held a delicate position in the racially stratified social hierarchy. They were seen as agents of colonizers, and exploiters in the colonial Africa. The native Africans' revulsion for them finds expression in widely read works like Kenyan writer Ngugi wa Thiongo's *The Trial of Dedan Kimathi*. The Indian character in the play, a symbolic representative of the class, is a deceitful, slimy, middleman who is negotiating on behalf of the White Man.

The doubly hyphenated diasporans are products of distinct cultural histories. The racial consciousness of East African Indians is different from that of the Indians. The former are products of complex race relations where they were viewed as collaborators and agents of the colonizers. The latter are products of an oppressive colonial system. The latter exhibit the "double consciousness" (W.E.B. Du Bois) where the racially oppressed race faces the psychological challenge of "always looking at one's self through the eyes" of a racist white society, and "measuring oneself by the means of a nation that looked back in contempt' (http://en.m.wikipedia.org/wiki/Double_consciousness). If racism is seen as propagating the ideas of high and low, developed and underdeveloped, superior and inferior, the later saw themselves as belonging to the second category while the former occupied the in-between space in this binary.

Consequently, there is a difference in response to racism between the works from the singly and doubly hyphenated writers. The mother in *Touch of Pink* dismisses it by reversing the racial gaze. She indulges in making racist comments on Giles, Amin's British boyfriend. Ian Iqbal Rashid is aware and critical of the White gaze as he points it out in the short film *Surviving Sabu*. His response to racism is more critical and composed than emotional and enraged. He expressed that in the poem *An/other Country* when the gay couple is watching *The Jewel in the Crown*:

> Now I watch you watch Sergeant Merrick watch poor Hari Kumar./ And follow as the white man's desire is twisted,/ manipulated into a beating. . . . My beauty is branded into the colour of my skin,/ my strands of hair thick as snakes,/ damp with the lushness of all the tropics,/ My humble penis cheated by the imperial wealth of yours./ Hari's corporal punishment, mine corporeal:/ Yet this is also part of my desire. (Sen 277)

This distinctive response to racism is a product of their distinctive socio-cultural history.

> It has occurred to me—how can it not?—that my picture of my past could well have, like the stories of my grandfather, acquired the patina of nostalgia, become idealized. But then, I have to convince myself, perhaps a greater and conscious discipline and the practice of writing mitigate that danger. I do carry my album of photos with me and my acquired newspaper cuttings and other assorted material, and there is always Deepa to check facts with. Still, what can

> ultimately withstand the cruel treachery of time, even as one tries to undermine it? (Qtd. Margitte, https://www.goodreads.com/review/show/1258740463)

The narrator in Vassanji's *The In-Between World of Vikram Lall* addresses the question of authenticity and texture of the diasporic fiction by the twice displaced writers. It echoes Rushdie's well-known statement, "What's the use of stories that aren't true?" (*Haroun and the Sea of Stories*). The narratives might not be 'true' but tell us how they wish to be identified at personal and collective levels.

The one event which connects the collective memory and shapes the lives and identities of the members of this diasporic community is the 1972 expulsion order by General Idi Amin, a product of the 'rage' of the native Africans. The fear and tragic experience of being forcefully exiled; the lived experience of belonging to multiple cultures; the experience of dislocation and relocation of 'home' are some of the markers of their collective memory and identity. They have experienced the fruits of colonisation; witnessed the process of postcolonization (independence struggle and building of national identity) without being a core part of it[15]; experienced the highs of being successful and the lows of being refugees; have called multiple locations as the true home. The narratives which emerge from the richness of experience of this group have the potential of giving new cultural language to survive in the truly globalized and transnational world.

To borrow Benedict Anderson's concept, if nations are "imagined communities," narratives from popular culture shape that imagination. The process of imagining is continuous and dynamic. Certain ideas, cultural practices and images are circulated in the popular culture which help shape this imaginary. The narratives of the diasporic community have a role to play in the imagining of nation.

The literature of the New (singly hyphenated) Diaspora has a complex relationship with the idea of nation for both the host and the homeland. First, for the host country, they maintain the binary of the "belonging absolutely" and "belonging" intact. Secondly, the literature provides superficial understanding of the culture and concerns of the diasporic community. If culture has a 'body' and a 'soul,' this literature engages itself with the superficial markers of the Indian culture. It gives enough familiarity to the majority to deal with the 'Otherness' and exploit the information for political and economic gains. Thirdly, and rarely, it contributes towards radicalization of a group in the homeland.

Contrary to this, the doubly displaced diasporic writing dilutes and truly de-territorializes the idea of belonging. The possibility of belonging to multiple cultures and geographical places is seen as a reality. Vassanji is moved by Tanzanian national anthem; wishes to explore the homeland of his ancestors, Gujarat; but Toronto is home. Yasmin Ladha equates home to a 'lover,' 'a place of re-departure' (*Aaj Savere)*.

The identity is a true hybrid. It is fractured. The influences are multiple. Some diasporic imaginary struggles to find coherence and other celebrates the multi-dimensional nature of the same. The members of Indian-East African diaspora belong to different Indian sub-cultures, speak different languages, worship different gods in different ways. The trauma of 1972 exodus may be a common point in the lives, and unique to them but the journey ahead is distinct again. The third homeland has treated them differently. It is the unique, distinct nature of their history—personal and collective—which gives a distinct flavour to the body of narratives written and produced by them.

The cultural industry promotes the literature of the singly hyphenated diasporas as it serves a particular purpose for those in power. So predictable is the plot that in a discussion on 'literary vs popular novels' on TVO (https://youtu.be/TtrWe1YaJNk), diaspora literature is referred to as "genre literature." Chitra Banerjee Divakaruni in an interview accepts that the editors are "always concerned about the market place. They want books to sell. . . . I have to always present like a little marketing plan." (http://thoughtfulindia.com)

However, it is the narratives emerging from the communities like East African Indians which have the power to give new parameters of identity, present alternate ways to look at race, citizenship and the idea of belonging. They have the potential to respond to the chants of "go back" in a highly blinkered world reality today.

NOTES

1. "Unfixed self" is a phrase used by Ramabai Espinet, a Trinidad born, Canada-based writer of Indian Diaspora. The phrase refers to the twice-displaced, hypermobile diasporic identities. It brings forth the question of the dynamics of belonging to multiple cultures.
2. It finds mention in *Periplus of the Erythraean Sea* written by a Greek pilot in 1st century. Lal, 254.
3. Whereas 'old' diaspora is a product of early capitalism, the 'new' one is associated with the 'movement of late capitalism.'
4. The "genre" literature written by the writers of Indian Diaspora which is produced and circulated in the market. As argued later in the paper, it fulfils a certain space in the political and cultural discourse of the nation state.
5. Important studies on 'Old' and 'New' diaspora include studies by Vijay Mishra (1995), Ravindra K. Jain (2004) and the paper uses the two categories in the same sense.
6. There are immigrants who have not come as indentured labourers. However, most fictional narratives use this as a narrative trope as majority did. This remains the most received reason for the presence of the 'Old' Diaspora in the collective perception.
7. This is the representation in the dominant narratives. There are studies which challenge this reading. Peter Simatei has argued that the very act of writing about the Asians in the national histories of resistance challenge the stereotype of Asians as collaborators of the British in official discourse of nation building. (2011: 56-67)

8. Discussed by Charles Ambler in a review of Sana Aiyar's book (519). http://iproxy.inflibnet.ac.in:2096/stable/44723399
9. J.M. Nazareth, *To The African: No guest am I*, http: www.google.com/amp/s/www.livemint.com/mint-lounge/features/the-in-between-world-of-the-african-goans/amp-1555659088733.
10. Britain closed its door to the Indian migrants whose parents or grandparents were not born in Britain. Between 1969-72, Britain was forced to take in some more migrants. They have a quota system of 1500 families per year.
11. RR7238A. Britain: Accommodating The Ugandan Asians (AP Archive) http://youtu.be/z4uKMT1gXOo published on 22 July 2015.
12. Rewind: Ugandan Canadians, CBC radio, November 24, 2016. https://www.cbc.ca/radio/rewind/1972-ugandan-refugees-an-honourable-place-in-canada-1.3860296
13. Interview conducted by "Penguin Random House Canada," 5 Oct. 2007, http://www.booklounge.ca/catalog/diaspora
14. May Joseph in *Nomadic Identities* discusses this idea and underscores the performative nature of citizenship.
15. This is debatable. Carl Rosenberg and John Nottingham in *The Myth of Mau Mau: Nationalism in Kenya* (1996) see the role played by the Indians in the Nationalist history of Kenya as "marginal" whereas historians like Sana Aiyar underscore "the deep political engagement of a diasporic Indian community with anticolonial nationalist movements in both Kenya and India" [*AHR*, vol. 116, No. 4, 2011] pp. 987-1013. However even Aiyar looks at the relationship between Indians and Africans as "tense and ambiguous." Aiyar maintains that "the colony's Indians, occupying a space between rebellion and loyalty, were simultaneously involved in supporting and suppressing Mau Mau." Post-independence, the Indians were further marginalized and by 1970, "one-third of Kenya's Indians had migrated to Britain." (Aiyar 2015)

Works Cited

Ambler, C. *The International Journal of African Historical Studies*, 48: 3, 2015.

Aiyar, Sana. "Anticolonial Homelands across the Indian Ocean: The Politics of the Indian Diaspora in Kenya, ca. 1930-1950," *The American Historical Review*, 2011, 116: 4.

_____. *Indians in Kenya: The Politics of Diaspora.* US: Harvard University Press, 2015.

A P Archive, RR7238A. *Britain: Accommodating The Ugandan Asians.* http://youtu.be/z4uKMT1gXOo, 22 July 2015.

Dimbleby, Johnathan. *Asian Expulsion.* 1972. UK: Thames TV.

Kalra, Kaur, Hutynuk. *Diaspora and Hybridity.* London: Sage, 2005.

Lal, Brij V., et al. *The Encyclopedia of the India Diaspora.* Singapore: Didier Millet, 2006.

Mishra, Vijay. *The Literature of the Indian Diaspora: Theorizing the Diasporic Imaginary*, London, New York: Routledge, 2007.

_____. *The Diasporic Imaginary and the Indian Diaspora.* New Zealand: Asian Studies Institute, 2005.

Nair, Meera, *My Own Country.* US: Showtime Ent. 2000.

_____, *Mississippi Masala.* US: Nair and Studio Canal Souss, 1992.

Nazareth, Peter. 2013. *The General is Up.* Goa: Goa1556. 2013

Pande, Amba. "Conceptualizing Indian Diaspora: Diversities within a Common Identity." *Economic and Political Weekly*, 48: 49 (2013): 59-65.

Rashid, Ian Iqbal (written and directed), *Touch of Pink.* UK, Canada: Sony Pictures Classics. 2004.

Safran, William. 1991 "Diasporas in Modern Societies: Myths of Homeland and Return," *Diaspora: A Journal of Transnational Studies*, 1: 1, Spring 1991. Toronto: University of Toronto Press.

Sen, Sudeep. 1994 "New Indian Poetry: The 1990s Perspective," *World Literature Today*, 68: 2, Spring 1994.

Simatei, Peter. "Diasporic Memories and National Histories in East African Asian Writing." *Research in African Literatures*, 42: 3, 2011.

Vassanji, M.G. *The In-Between World of Vikram Lall.* Vintage Contemporaries, 2005.

https://www.cbc.ca/radio/rewind/1972-ugandan-refugees-an-honourable-place-in-canada-1.3860296 [1]

http://www.google.com/amp/s/www.livemint.com/mint-lounge/features/the-in-between-world-of-the-african-goans/amp-1555659088733.html

Diaspora Literature

SANGEETHA GORAK
Res. Sch., Kakatiya University, Warangal

Indian Diaspora occupies second largest place in the world; around 25 million all over the world. Diasporic writing occupies a significant place. Diasporic literature focuses on themes like discrimination, cultural shock and reverse cultural shock, problems in adjustment and assimilation, orientalism, identity crisis, alienation and displacement, dilemma, depression, hybridity and generation gap.

Diaspora term was coined from Greek 'Dia' (means across), 'Sporien' (means to sow or to scatter seeds). It was used by the ancient Greeks for citizens of a dominant state who emigrate to a conquered land with the purpose of colonization, to assimilate the territory into the empire. Later it was used with reference to the Jews who lived most of the time as 'diaspora' people. Diaspora is simply the displacement of community or culture into another geographical and cultural region. A simple explanation of diaspora literature, then, would be works that are written by writers who live outside their native land. The term recognizes a work's characteristic geographic origins.

Diaspora literature may also be defined by its contents, irrespective of where it was written. For instance, the story of Joseph (Gen 37-50) is frequently called a "diaspora story" because although its final form was written within the land of Israel, it explains how Joseph learns to survive outside his homeland. *The Book of Job* is another example of diaspora literature because it was written in the wake of the Babylonian damage, which gave rise to the question, why God punished Israel, the chosen people, with such mass suffering.

The term diaspora comes from the Greek translation of the *Hebrew Bible*, particularly Deut 28:25. This translation was called the Septuagint and it was the project of Greek-speaking Jews who lived in the Egyptian diaspora. The entire Septuagint could be described as diaspora literature, as it is the work of Jews living outside their homeland—and their translation reflects that orientation. But specific books such as the books of Tobit and Judith, which feature Jewish protagonists living outside the land or under foreign domination and which reflect on how the Jews might survive in this situation, are described as diasporic because of their contents and concerns. Diasporic literature may be aware of the ancestral native land, but the nostalgia for it has lessened, if not disappeared. And diasporic literature is, moreover, engaged by the possibilities of the new location. Finally, it may be written well after the Babylonian exile by Jews who decided not to return. Diasporic living stops short of integration because the community still maintains its distinctive identity and its status as a minority people. There are various types of Diaspora.

1. Religious diaspora is the biblical diaspora of the exodus of the Jews.
2. Secular diaspora is of different kinds.

   A: Victim diaspora: A class of people who have been banished from their place of origin and sent to another land. Usually a result of a traumatic event like conquest, persecution, enslavement and genocide or exile, e.g. Africans in the North Atlantic Slave trade.

   B: Trading diaspora: A community, often members of an extended family, that goes abroad to conduct trade in host society. They receive permission from the host govt., learn local language and customs, but do not assimilate. E.g.: Jews, Chinese, Arabs, Indians, Armenians.

C: Imperial diaspora: Migrants who go to another land that has been conquered by their own nation and enjoy higher status on account of their ethnic ties to the ruling power. They do not adapt to customs but locals adapt to their customs, e.g. The Spanish and the Indians, Mexico's caste system.

D: Labour diaspora: Indentured servants and labour migrants, e.g. Colonial America.

During ancient period, lot of Indians migrated to Far East and South East Asia to spread Buddhism.

Diaspora is commonly divided in two phases, Old diaspora (colonial period) and New diaspora (postcolonial period). In the South Asian context, the old diaspora is the time during the colonial period, from 1830 to 1930 when there was British rule. In Indian region, the colonial phase started in 19th century and continued up to 20th century. In the colonial phase diaspora mainly indicates only those immigrants who were taken from India to British colonies such as Fiji, Surinam and other French colonies. Old diaspora had not given any chance to the people and they were uprooted. The chance to go back to their homeland was very less. In this phase, the migration was a history of misery, deprivation and sorrow. According to Gayatri Chakravorty Spivak: "The old diaspora was the result of war, religious non secular oppression, slavery and trade," since the nineteenth century and the new diaspora is "the new scattering of the seeds of 'developing' nations." (246)

In the nineteenth century, migration was due to industrialization and developed economics. During this period, people willingly migrated to other lands for higher education and better prospects. However, the nostalgia for native language, culture, food and traditions results in a dilemma of identity and clash of culture.

Diaspora writers took solace in writing and won accolades for their work. The works of early diaspora writers are autobiographic and focus on the problems like nostalgia, rootlessness, homelessness, dislocation and displacement. There is a loss of home land and gain of new host land.

There are two moves of the diasporic writers. The Temporal move involves a look backward to the past and a look forward at the future. It describes nostalgia, themes of survival, and themes of cultural assimilation. The Spatial move involves a deterritorialization and reterritorialization connected by journey. Diasporic expertise comes from a memory of loss, of leaving the home, of not having any soul connection with the host country and acts as a sort of a bridge between two different cultures.

V.S Naipaul was born in the small town of Chaguanas on the Island of Trinidad. The sense of "Homelessness" came naturally to him. *A House for Mr. Biswas* presents his recollections of childhood. Mr. Biswas's life is very similar to the life of Naipaul. Mr. Biswas's search of a new 'house' is a search for belonging that he is not the 'other' to possess a place in an alien land. The diasporic sensibility shows in his writing.

Amitav Ghosh, another author of Indian Diaspora, was born in Calcutta. He later shifted to Delhi for higher studies and currently lives in New York. In 2008, he published his famous novel *Sea of Poppies*. The first part of the novel deals with the colonial period of India; it has the descriptions of migration of indentured labourers who left their land never to return and to settle in a foreign country where they could not find their self-identity.

Jhumpa Lahiri portrays in her novels the crisis of identity and belongingness. Lahiri was born on July 11, 1967 in London and later her family shifted to the United States. Her novel *The Namesake* presents the life of Gogol Ganguli, the American born son of Ashoka and Ashima Ganguli. Gogol swings between the Indian culture and American culture. He is an ABCD, an "America born confused desi," who doesn't have the answer to the question, "where are you from?" He knows that his parents and their friends refer to India simply as "desh." Even though Gogol never thinks of India as his desh, he feels himself alien in America. At the end of the novel, he realizes his heritage and the value of his Indian identity. *The Namesake* gives a deep insight into the immigrant's families who make every effort to inculcate in their children the cultural and ethical values of their native country. It also deals with the misery of the children who have to deal with two different cultures.

Another important diaspora writer is Anita Desai. Her novel *Bye-Bye Blackbird* is about migrant Indians in the England of the 1960s. Anita Desai's *Fasting, Feasting* is a novel of distinction between two cultures: the one Indian, known for its pious and ancient customs representing fasting; and the other American, known for its opulence and sumptuousness epitomizing feasting. Arun in *Fasting, Feasting* is an excellent example of an Indian in the suburbs of Massachusetts, finding himself lonely and unable to adjust to a culture of freedom.

The Inheritance of Loss is the novel by Indian diaspora author Kiran Desai. Through Jemubhai's life, she shows how race discrimination can influence and harm an innocent and naive young man. The turning point in Jemubhai's life comes in 1939, when he goes to Cambridge, England, to study. During this time he learns what hate and racism are.

1. They retain a collective memory, vision, or myth about their original homeland—its physical location, history, and achievements and, often enough, sufferings.
2. They believe that they are not, and perhaps cannot be, fully accepted by their host society and therefore feel partly alienated and insulated from it.
3. They continue to relate, personally or vicariously, to that homeland in one way or another, and their ethno-communal consciousness and solidarity are importantly defined in terms of the existence of such a relationship. The absence of such a relationship makes it difficult to speak of transnationalism.
4. In structuring their communities and adapting to their host lands, diasporas become themselves independent centers of

cultural creation; yet their creations continue to contain certain ethno-symbols, customs, and narratives of the homeland.

5. Their cultural, religious, economic, and/or political relationships with the homeland are reflected in a significant way in their communal institutions.

Salman Rushdie is a famous diaspora author; he was born in Bombay; in 1967 his parents shifted to Pakistan. He completed his higher studies in Britain. In his novel *Midnight's Children*, Rushdie shows the anguish of displacement. In Pakistan, Saleem comments: "I left my lifelong home." (394) As a result, "his body goes numb, the only sense active is his sense of smell, like a dog, anaesthetized against feeling as well as memories." (493) His loss of memory leads to the creation of a new identity in Pakistan. Hence, he becomes a member of the Cutia Unit. One of his fellow soldiers starts calling him 'Buddha' because "there hung around him an air of great antiquity." (287) Here Saleem Sinai is presented as a symbol of the diaspora who face difficulty in the newly inhabited countries.

Midnight's Children depicts life of Salim Sinai in the background of India's political history. It deals with India's transition from British colonialism to independence and the partition of India. The novel moves from Kashmir to Amritsar massacre, and democratic India with Nehru as first prime minister, riots of the 1950s, the Indo-China war of 1962, the Indo-Pakistan war of 1971 and the emergency imposed by Indira Gandhi in 1975.

Saleem Sinai was born at the exact moment when India became an independent country. Saleem notices that all children born in India between midnight to 1 a.m. on 15 August 1947 are imbued with extraordinary telepathic powers. Saleem has hybrid identity; he was an illegal child of William Methwold, a British who left India on the day British raj ended, and Vanita, a Hindu. When he was born, he was swapped by the nurse Mary Pereira and brought up in a Muslim family.

Saleem journeys through India, Pakistan and Bangladesh and yet there is no place for him to settle down. About writing the novel, Rushdie says: "what I was actually doing was a novel of memory and about memory, so that my India was just that: it is 'my' India, a version and no more than one version of all the hundreds of millions of versions." (10)

When Saleem goes to Pakistan, he feels lonely. When his parents say: "We must all become new people in the land of the pure, purity became our ideal. Then Saleem has forever tainted with Bombayness, his head was full of all sorts of religions separately from Allah's." (431) In Pakistan, Saleem thinks: "not even learning could make me feel a part of this country devoid of midnight's children." (431) Saleem lives away from midnight's children and India. Like Rushdie, Saleem does not feel at home in Pakistan. Rushdie has also exposed the condition of Muslims after independence in India through some Muslim characters. Narlikar opines, "freeze a Muslim's assets, they say, and you make him run to Pakistan, leaving all his wealth behind him" (185). Muslims feel that the Indian government wants all Muslims to go to Pakistan. In the novel, Saleem's mother says, "What is left in this India? . . . Go, leave it all, go to Pakistan." (189) After partition, the Muslims are in dilemma whether to stay in India or go to Pakistan because those who migrated from India are treated as second grade citizens in Pakistan.

Saleem's story represents plural identities of Indian Muslims which resulted from the feeling of being in exile and consequently there is a fragmented search for identity through memory. Through him, the novelist tries to restore a link between the migrants and their original homeland through narration and description and through their desire for 'home' with an effort to establish their identity. Rushdie explores the life of an immigrant and tries to solve the mystery of "who am I?" Rushdie introduced in his novel mainly protagonist's alienation, Indian culture, the political scenario of Indian subcontinent, history and fantasy.

Diasporic literature deals with the sense of loss and alienation. It addresses problems related to amalgamation or disintegration of cultures. The migrants suffer from the pain of being far their homes and the anguish of leaving behind everything familiar. Diaspora writings have cast a new aura around global India and contributed in building a new image of India abroad. Diaspora writing supports strengthening bonds between various countries through historical, cultural, social, traditional and economic ties.

Works Cited

Bhabha, Homi K. *The Location of Culture*. London: Routledge, 1994.

Dhawan, R.K. *Writers of the Indian Diaspora*. New Delhi: Prestige, 2001.

Herwitz, Daniel and Ashutosh Varshney. *Midnight's Diaspora: Encounters with Salman Rushdie*. New Delhi: Penguin, 2009.

Jayaram, N., ed. "Introduction: The Study of Indian Diaspora," *The Indian Diaspora: Dynamics of Migration*. New Delhi: Sage, 2004.

Martien A. Halvorson-Taylor, "Diaspora Literature," http://www.bibleodyssey.org/en/people/related-articles/diaspora-literature

Pandey, Abhay. *Indian Diasporic Literature*. New Delhi: Creative. 2008.

Paranjape, M. *Indian Diaspora: Theories, Texts, Histories*. Delhi: Indianlog, 2001.

Rushdie, Salman. *Midnight's Children*. New York: Penguin, 1991.

Spivak, Gayatri Chakravarty. *In Other Worlds: Essays in Cultural Politics*. New York: Methuen, 1987.

Diasporic Element in Jhumpa Lahiri's "Interpreter of Maladies"

SHAHNAZ
St. Joseph's Degree College, Kurnool

Diasporic literature is a broad term which refers to the writings of the authors who stay outside their native land but their writings are associated with the customs and culture of their native land. It deals with concepts like alienation, displacement, nostalgia, quest for identity and rootlessness. It also addresses the issues that are often related to amalgamation of the culture of the host land. Uma Parameswaran writes about this diasporic condition: "First is nostalgia for the homeland left behind mingled with fear in a strange land. The second is a phase in which one is busy adjusting to the new environment that there is little creative output. The third phase is the shaping of diaspora existence by involving themselves in ethno-cultural issues. The fourth is when they have arrived and start participating in the larger world of politics and national issues."

Similar views have been expressed by William Safran: "They continue to relate personally or vicariously, to the homeland in a way or another, and their ethno-communal consciousness and solidarity are importantly defined by the existence of such a relationship." Thus, diaspora refers to the mass dispersion of involuntary nature as they are compelled to move out of their native lands for multiple reasons.

In the words of Robin Cohen, the features of diaspora are: dispersal from native land; sometimes, the expulsion from homeland in search of work, in pursuit of trade or to further colonial ambitions. Diaspora can be a collective memory and myth about the homeland; or visualizing ideal image for the ancestral land. It sometimes speaks of conflict with the societies of host land. It can be a strong ethic group consciousness sustained over a long time.

Writers of Indian diaspora try to relocate themselves in the culture of host land. During this struggle to assimilate, their minds oscillate between dislocation and relocation. This situation is compared to the concept of 'Trishanku Swarga' in the *Ramayana*. It is an apt term to describe the predicament of the expatriate writers. Feroza Jussawalla comments: "We are like chiffon saris—a sort of cross-breed attempt to adjust to pressures of a new world while actually being from an older one." (583-95)

Dislocation can be defined as a disconnection with ancestral land and its identity. The immigrants feel lonely and alienated when they are not accepted by the host society which often results in ethnic discrimination. Their strong and deep-rooted native culture results in picturing their homeland to be heavenly and they yearn to visit their ancestral lands. The immigrant writers derive satisfaction by portraying their fancied homeland in their work.

The diasporic writings are of two types: Literature on the diaspora and Literature of/ by the diaspora. Diasporic literature focuses on the concepts of location, dislocation and relocation. Men of letters like T.S. Eliot, Sylvia Plath, Ezra Pound, W.H. Auden, Seamus Heaney immigrated from their homeland and struggled hard to relocate themselves. V.S. Naipaul, Rohinton Mistry, Shiva Naipaul, Sam Selvon, M.G. Vassanji and Subramaniam belong to the first generation of Indian diasporic writers. Meera Syal, Shashi Tharoor, Hari Kunzru, Sunetra Gupta and Jhumpa Lahiri belong to the second generation.

The present paper focuses on the title story in Jhumpa Lahiri's *Interpreter of Maladies* which won Pulitzer award in 1999. This collection of short stories focuses on diasporic sensibility. In the title story, Mr. Das, along with his family, pays a visit to India to meet his parents. They set out to visit Konark, a historic monument. To go there. they hire a taxi and Mr. Kapasi is their guide. Mr. Das's family consists of his wife Mina and three children, two boys and a girl. During their travel, they have a conversation with Kapasi and learn that earlier he used to work as an interpreter in the clinic of a doctor, most of whose patients spoke Gujarati. He translates their maladies to the doctor. This profession as an interpreter of maladies is elevated by Mrs. Das. Her appreciation of this profession shocks Mr. Kapasi since he found nothing extraordinary and exceptional in that vocation. His wife considered the job menial, as he was a subordinate to the doctor. The appreciation of Mr. Das draws Kapasi to her and he starts visualising a romantic bond with her. He feels further encouraged when Mr. Das and Mrs. Das ask him to join them in their family photo. Then Mrs. Das asked Mr. Kapasi his postal address to mail the prints of the photos. Mr. Kapasi begins imagining romantic correspondence with Mrs. Das. But this dream is shattered when Mrs. Das asks him to interpret her malady that was haunting her for eight years. The sense of guilt burdened her and she could not establish a healthy relationship with her husband and children. She confessed having an extramarital relationship with Mr. Das's Punjabi friend. Bobby, one of her two sons, was a product of this relationship. Mr. Kapasi is shocked to learn this: "All he can utter is, 'Is it really pain you feel, Mrs. Das or is it, guilt?'" (55) Kapasi fails to provide any solace to Mrs. Das. Rather, his question pushes her into eternal silence. Mr. Kapasi here represents the patriarchal society.

The second paragraph of the story hints at the struggle of Indian Americans to relocate themselves in the host land: "The family looked Indian but dressed as foreigners did, the children in stiff brightly coloured clothing." Anupama Kaushal says: "The writings of Jhumpa Lahiri are all about such diasporic Bengali migrants settled in USA. She is fortunately among those writers who have become aware of the relativity of the concept of diaspora, its contradiction, numerous possibilities of alienation and assimilation, going back to various patterns of memory, the marginal and the central—which all we observe in her Pulitzer Prize-winning fiction *Interpreter of Maladies*. The collection of short stories talks not only about the contradictions, complexities and ambivalences of Bengali diaspora in Boston but also of diaspora prevalent within the nation and even in one's own house. It is largely about those who are associated with shifting from one society and adjusting into another." (92)

The silence of Mrs. Das speaks volumes about the cultural conflict; an extra-marital affair is accepted in America, and Mrs. Das would have taken it in a lighter vein as she was living there since birth. Abha Shukla comments on the dilemmatic plight of the immigrants: "Lahiri's characters reflect traces of India through the details of characters who inhabit the complex and complicated world of Indian immigrants in the United States. Her characters seem to exist simultaneously in two cultures; the reality of American experience and the memories and sphere of Indian traditions." (58)

Apart from this, the story "Interpreter of Maladies" enhances the definition of diaspora, a feeling of displacement, that it need not be to only takes place when the people are culturally uprooted, but it also can be one's own family. There are lot of similarities between Mrs. Das and Mr. Kapasi though they belong to different cultural background. Even in her home she feels herself to be alienated for the guilt of having established an extramarital affair with the friend of her husband some eight years ago. And she could not share this to none as she belongs to the second generation of immigrants who are completely disconnected and uprooted from the home land. And she made the futile attempt to ease herself from the stress that has overburdened her for eight years. It can be understood form her conversation with Mr. Kapasi whom she thought to give remedy:

> Don't you see? For eight years I haven't been able to express this to anybody, not to friends, certainly not to Raj. He doesn't even suspect

> it. . . . I feel terrible looking at my children and at Raj always terrible. I have terrible urges. Mr. Kapasi, to throw things away. One day, I had the urge to throw everything. Don't you think it is unhealthy? (55)

Even Mr. Kapasi, in spite of being deeply rooted in his family, experiences the feelings of displacement and alienation which unfortunately lead to the death of his son due to typhoid. One can conclude that displacement need not always be cultural; it can be also in one's very home.

Works Cited

Bala, Suman, ed. *Jhumpa Lahiri: The Master Storyteller*. New Delhi: Khosla, 1999.

_____, ed. *Jhumpa Lahiri*. New Delhi:

Dhawan, R.K. ed. *Writers of the Indian Diaspora*. New Delhi: Prestige, 2001.

Kaushal, Anupama. In *The Literature of Indian Diaspora*, ed. T.S Anand. New Delhi: Creative, 2010, p. 92.

Lahiri, Jhumpa. *Interpreter of Maladies*. New Delhi: Harper Collins, 1999.

Shukla-Kaushik, Abha. "Diaspora, and Cross-cultural Identity: A Study of Jhumpa Lahiri's Fictional Works," *Women Writers of Indian Diaspora*, ed. Silky Kumar Anand, New Delhi: Creative, 2010.

Chowdhury, Anupama. "*Interpreters of Maladies*: A Saga of Diaspora and Multiculturalism," *The Journal of Indian Writing in English*, 37.1 (Jan. 2009), pp. 1224.

Bridging the 'Home and Everywhere Else': Meera Syal's *Life isn't all ha ha hee hee*

MADHURI CHAWLA
Dyal Singh Evening College, University of Delhi

The identity of an individual has both a collective and a personal dimension. It is moulded by the sensitivity towards the surrounding world including race, religion, class and creed. Further, economic and social well-being of the family, cultural norms and religious convictions shared by the society in which the individual grows up also contribute to the identity formation of the individual. The individual consciousness is thus a composite of both a group identity as well as an individual identity.

When the individual relocates from the place of origin to an adopted country, the entire gamut of the convictions, customs, norms of the place of origin, popularly called the 'socio-cultural baggage' follow the immigrant to the nation of adoption. Salman Rushdie, in his *Imaginary Homelands*, a collection of essays spanning from 1981 to 1991, states that the immigrants haunted by a sense of loss and driven by an urge to reclaim the lost world look back and merely recreate what was lost, and what they recreate is far removed from the real. He calls these "imaginary homelands" (10). In a bid to construct these 'imaginary homelands' the translocated individual desperately clings to his native way of life as a protective gear in an alien setting through the constituent markers of identity like attire, cooking, language, religion, customs and ceremonies, and so forth. The shedding off of, or holding on to the social markers is subject to factors like the time of dislocation of the immigrant as also upon the area to which he relocates. Furthermore, it also varies from one individual to another as does the conflict and dilemma faced. Factors like the individuals' education, economic condition, and so on make the networks even within a given region profoundly dissimilar. Furthermore, the distinction in the historical dynamics responsible for their relocation additionally assume a significant part in identity formation of the diasporic individual. Diaspora, therefore, can't be perceived as a homogeneous and coherent cluster. It is not a monolithic chunk.

Santosh Sareen in *A Home Everywhere: The Consciousness of Diasporic Belonging*, contends that diaspora is impacted by the socio-cultural variations among themselves as also by the culture of the adopted land. He says that the constituent markers of identity like food, attire, language retention, religion, music, dance, myths, legends, customs, rituals, and so forth are retained, discarded or adopted differently at different times and places, and yet the pull of the roots persists for years and sometimes centuries (89). Therefore, the lumping together of individuals of various character and considering that their identities are static, would be deluding.

Safran, Cohen, Sheffer, Medan and Bruneau each fostered their own individual arrangements of "common features" of a diaspora to deal with the plurality of the term diaspora. Scholars consequently have over the course of the years attempted to characterize Diaspora differently, in some cases clubbing them under one umbrella and on occasion separating them into sub-categories. Anthias, in his article, "Evaluating 'Diaspora': Beyond Ethnicity," likewise says that the diasporas are not monolithic, and as such diasporic discourse should not buy in to an "absolutist" idea of "Origin"; they also have layers, and hence, researchers should also focus on internal variations within an ethnic group. However much one may attempt to frame broad criterion and gauges to arrive at a fixed notion of Diaspora, the fact remains that even within a specific diaspora no two encounters can be comparative experiences. So, despite the fact that the Indian diaspora 'scattered' in different parts of the world shares a typical social legacy and a profound feeling of connectedness with India, yet it is a diverse and heterogeneous community demonstrating varied dialects, social and cultural beliefs etc. Meera Syal in an interview with Jonathan Owen, too rankles at the way she and others are corralled together as "Asian." "It's one of those awkward umbrella terms that's increasingly losing relevance," she says. "We're not just one homogenous lump"

Her *Life isn't all ha ha hee hee* (1999), a women-centric novel, plays on this idea. Syal explores the specificities of women's experiences, a further subdivision within a community, and as Jennifer Reese of *The New York Times* says she manages "to get inside the heads of three very different characters, inspiring sympathy for both tricky, adulterous sirens and sari-clad housewives." The narrative gives voice to the three second generation young diasporic women of Punjabi community as it brings forth the point that while identity has collective dimensions reflected through Race, Gender, Ethnicity etc., it is also individual and is subject to singular decisions and personality traits.

The narrative takes us through the lives of these three childhood friends, Tania, Sunita and Chila, the cultural cross-currents they are forced to face as also the conflict that it leads to in their lives. Syal, herself a second-generation immigrant, in the novel through the girls chronicles a tale fraught with conflict, both internal and external, of female bonding, of patriarchal expectations, of biases and of how the three women reject those expectations, and chart their own separate trajectories. It delineates the alternatives available to diasporic Indian women in relation to their cultures of origin and that of their adoption. Their families who are first generation immigrants try to inculcate in them the cultural values and habits of the community. These custodians of the values of the native land have an unashamed pride in their own culture and a condescending attitude towards the culture of the host land. They tenaciously hold on to the norms of religion, marriage and other customs, wear traditional clothes and prefer Indian spouses for their children and make all efforts to find suitable matches for the three girls within their community. Leading by and large an insular life, they are happy and comfortable in their cocooned existence, their own space and zone in this foreign land.

The three friends born in the land of adoption like all second-generation immigrants are brought up on a steady diet of Indian values and culture at home; subjected to oppression at the hands of patriarchal norms carried over from the homeland, a value system in which docility and domesticity, virginity and chastity continue to be the norm for girls. Tania's mother starts her preparation early, training her how to be unnoticeable, to be sensitive to everybody's mood, and so on. However, she does liberate Tania from the drudgery of cooking, cleaning, and shopping as she feels Tania would need to do that for her entire life and hence must enjoy her life now. Sunita's mother believes firmly that sticking around Wills Fish Bar excessively would amount to the girls catching the "English disease" of divorce, along with "short skirts, bad skin and bland food" (81). Divorce amongst the Punjabis is a stigma for the woman, and divorced women are considered equitable to "shop soiled goods," they never get to remarry, while "men can always start again" (82) as Sunita's divorced auntie, whom Sunita calls "modern aunty," states. Sunita's mother conceals dowry and gold ornaments in her saree as a sort of "insurance" against any such exigency as that of the "modern aunty"; "just in case" as Sunita's mom puts it. Chila's folks attacked the marriage markets on all fronts: "the matrimonial bureaux where they find a perfect match by matching up your heights and income brackets, the notice boards in the temples and community centres where your personal details are displayed along with the times for yoga classes and the winner of the under-sevens trampolining competition, and, of course, the gossip grapevine" (148-49). Arranged marriages within their own community is the norm especially so for girls. The supposedly more progressive Sunita's family apparently give her the freedom to choose her own partner, but as in Gurinder Chadha's movie *Bend it Like Beckham* the freedom is restricted to "a Hindu Punjabi with prospects" (149) and project that it was "assisted" and there was no "arranging" in their home. And surprisingly the defiant Tania too is made to go through the process of 'groom hunting' by her mother.

The parents thus try to retain the Indian connect; however the extent to which the three girls relate to their country of origin, imbibe and follow its norms and value system, defines their life. Chila the docile and submissive one suppresses her own identity in favour of the one that society has fashioned for her. She seems to have imbibed the values fostered at home and apparently has to suffer the most, also on account of body shaming as she is apparently not beautiful, and has hardly any academic accomplishments to boast of. The appearance of the girl is always of paramount importance and the aunties, Chila's mother's friends, the self-proclaimed representatives of the conventional school of thought so religiously preserved and guarded in the host land had a constant mantra, "No man will ever want that one, the plump darkie with the shy stammer" (14) Tania's remark on the circumstance of her friend reveals how even in the "progressive" land the life of Punjabi women continues to be defined by the social ethos of the "roots." "Chila didn't have much choice. Coming from the most traditional family and obviously not college material, they were lining up boys for her before she left school. Ironic, really, that the girl who most wanted to Do the Right Thing was considered defective material" (148).

However, Chila the warm, slow and dark girl, who like Chaya in Baldwin's "Nothing Must Spoil This Visit," "hated upsetting people" and keeps quiet and keeps smiling, is rewarded by being chosen by Deepak, primarily because she fits into the mould of the conventional girl who, "will follow his lead in life" (14) and as Deepak thinks, "She is as sweet as the blossom outside my window, and just as virginal. . . . She doesn't need to prance around in thongs and halter necks, her beauty is beautiful because it's hidden and it will be mine" (12). Chila manages to marry Deepak, considered to be one of the most eligible bachelors in the community as Deepak too, a second-generation immigrant, stands firm on the belief that as a man he may have his numerous flings, but the Punjabi patriarchal belief of marrying a virgin continues to be an important concern when he chooses his bride.

Groomed as per convention Chila dedicates herself to domesticity and her trajectory seems headed towards a perfect married life. Nurtured and trained for marriage, Chila settles into matrimony with ease and comfort. However, when Tania who is a professional documentary filmmaker starts shooting a film about love and marriage among Indians in England, she casts her own friends including Chila as subjects. The film exposes the fissures in their lives as we watch Chila quickly and effortlessly learn to unlearn the lessons in docility and the narrative unfolds how she grows to seek recognition, something that no patriarchal handbook had trained her in. A slice of recognition and fame, makes her yearn for more of it. She no longer subscribes to the patriarchal norm that women must always maintain a facade of being happily married under all circumstances. The narrative goes on to unfold a metamorphosed Chila. Chila who is on family way discovers that her husband has rekindled his affair with his ex-flame, Tania, despite Chila's constant endeavour to be an ideal wife. She resolves to raise her son as a single parent and boldly decides to call it quits. The submissive and docile Chila comes into her own and decides to live life on her own terms. She sheds off the veneer her lifelong grooming has forced her to wear for the pleasure of others. Thus, a profoundly traditional Chila, a Chila whose "tomorrows were filled with, built around a Deepak" (160), evolves and transitions into a confident 'I,' liberating herself from the marital shackles making her own plans to take her son Anand to India, her home country alone, it felt 'new' and 'unfamiliar' but "It wasn't so bad to be here alone" she says as she attends Tania's father's funeral, "feeling light as air" (333).

The bold and confident Tania, the fiery Tans, right from the word go stands in total contrast to Chila. She is a non-conformist and a rebel right from the beginning, paying little heed to traditional sermons she throws docility to the winds. Influenced by the culture of the land of adoption, she disapproves of her mother for conforming to practices and customs that sustain the male sacrosanct. She remembers that her mother, "shrivelled to the size of a wrinkled pea around her husband," taught her daughter how to please others while "tak[ing] up as little room as possible." Tania battles against the pressures of the Indian community and is rejected by probable husbands including Deepak, lined up by her family who judge her as "too modern," "too Western," and "a bit of a slapper" or not ready to adjust to the closed community of Indian social life (150). The eastern ideology defined by collectivism, adhered to by her clan in the land of adoption, is too claustrophobic for her, as she has imbibed the individualistic values of the host land. Having grown up in a society which underscores what Hofstede says in his book, *Culture's Consequences: International Differences in Work-Related Issues,* the "I" consciousness, autonomy, emotional independence, individual initiative, right to privacy, pleasure seeking, financial security etc. she decides to remain single and be on her own. This also leads to rupture of relation from her traditional brother and his family. Seeking to free herself from the ethnic trap, she shuns the ghettoized Punjabi existence in London's East End and moves on to become a programme maker for television.

Tania the fast learner can see through patriarchy quite early; she is quick to break the mould and refuses to follow the prescribed path. She understands that her brother hates her so much for not following the trodden path; it's for what she hasn't done, "I haven't been at home, feeding everyone, supporting everyone, smiling at everyone, keeping the family going" (110). While the clever Tania can easily read the subtext of her own ethos, it also results in easy assimilation into the new world, and Tania finds the proximity of her community and its ethos too demanding. "The endless questions of who what why she was, to whom she belonged (father/ husband/ workplace), why her life wasn't following the ordained patterns for a woman of her age, religion, height and income bracket. The sheer physical effrontery of her people, wanting to be inside her head, to own her, claim her, preserve her. Her people" (15). Unlike Chila, she discerns the functioning of patriarchy like the back of her hand. Sunita visualising Tania's response, were she to be asked by a man to enter the flames for him like 'Sita,' rightly knows for sure that "Tania would push him in and add petrol for good measure. And then invite her mates round for a barbecue." (49) A woman of the world, she demonstrates grit as she protests and fights against established norms, ready to shoulder responsibility for her actions.

The "new woman," self-assured and self-reliant, she is conscious of the effect of her looks on men and Tania knows how to use it to her advantage. Subverting the accepted norms, she refuses to be acted upon, rather, unlike the traditional Punjabi women she is the one who acts. Her desire for freedom is not limited merely to achievement in the outside world, she is also the "man" in the house. She earns more than her live-in partner, Martin, who also keeps the house for her; the white boyfriend is the "domesticated" one catering to the household chores. This western identity is however also a construct. Tania does unconsciously relate with her Indian roots as is manifest when she wants Martin to call her "jaan," a Hindi endearment term. Again, apparently having broken loose from her "traditional moorings," Tania calls her friends, "the pindoos" (rustics) but Sunita notices that "Tania still sat like one with them, crossed legs, shoes off, unknotting herself in a way that suggested despite her protestations that part of her still responded to them like home" (18-19). When her estranged father is on the deathbed, the rebellious Tania yearns 'for goodness' 'for resolution' and is reminded of what her mum once told her about 'Karma,' thus traversing back in time and space to find solace in the philosophy of the homeland.

Chila and Tania are the two extremes while Sunita treads a path somewhere in between. Initially a radical, she gets easily manipulated into following the cultural norms as she settles into matrimony, an overweight depressed housewife. The divorcee

"Modern aunty" had enlightened a young and impressionable Sunita, helping her discern how in her Punjabi world, men had entered the house and sat, while the women stood to attention at their beck and call, serving them (82). Sunita observes how the same was true for her brothers as well who learnt from the example of their father. Though not the one to subserviently accept the male-female dynamics of the Indian community she does join the "Asian Soc out of a sense of duty" to seek out 'her brethren' and 'express her solidarity' but insists that "just because we shared the same skin tone, I didn't have to like them" (85). Later she gets "heavily involved with the Uni Women's Group" in her university championing the cause of women impressing the group with anecdotes about being reminded of coming "from a repressive culture in which women were treated as cattle." (87) advocating the idea of a "strong female" (87). Sunita the student was a feminist and an activist who questioned the validity of the conventional Indian ethos being imparted to her. Unlike the 'good women' of her community she was capable of cracking a dirty joke and Tania teasingly called her "a bad woman" (21) thereby implying that even Sunita was capable of decoding the social norms. Theoretically she was aware that rules are arbitrary and not integral and need not always regulate their lives.

The theoretically enlightened Sunita however is unable to realize her full potential and allows her wings to be clipped by Akash. Her activism seems limited to waving placards and wearing badges, but when it comes to life she constantly battles not to rebel, not to react to the bait of Akash's angry words. Having unconsciously imbibed the values of her ethos she is quick to understand in the first few years of her married life itself the subtext of Sita's trial through fire to prove her purity. She gives up everything and we soon find her plump, with a child "surgically attached" to her side. But her discontent with this unassuming, self-abnegating existence soon surfaces, as the 'other' in her asserts that she needs pay attention to herself, to take care of herself, to groom herself. Sunita who had completely lost herself in the household chores struggles to rediscover herself as she starts "putting unnatural colours" in her hair, going out a lot and coming back late" (242) challenges the conventional mores making a provocative choice by wearing a "bright red mini dress," there are spells in the day when she forgets she has two children and begins to spend "increasing amounts of time . . . with similarly badly behaved women" (242). She struggles as she strives to justify and to convince herself, "I do love my children and I always tried my best. . . . I have a life too, you know!" (244) Her yearning for her 'unconditioned self' surfaces as she moves out to work, to chalk out a life which allows for her own gratification as well. Silencing the voice of conditioning, she convinces herself that Akash will be able to manage the children in her absence. Sunita finally manages to bridge the gap between 'the home and the world' borrowing the title of Tagore's work, as we learn that she is working hard for her first-year exams and that Akash intends to whisk her away for a romantic holiday immediately afterwards.

Thus, we find that Syal locates unique female experiences through the three friends, as they negotiate their lives within the rigid norms their community lives by in the diasporic land, documenting the stereotyped binaries of angel/ devil, sati-Savitri/ kali. Their movement is from learning the tradition to unlearning the accepted and the unacceptable, traversing to arrive at the 'discovery of the self.' The paths traversed by the three protagonists in this narrative of the third space are similar yet different. The 'Trishanku' state of diaspora cannot be homogenized as a singular experience undiluted by other socio-cultural factors. Syal writes, "It was simple really, only having to choose between two worlds, home and everywhere else. And in between was the long walk home, and the three of us, rebuilding the crossing on each journey" (319). The journey between the 'home' and the 'everywhere else' as stated by Syal in the novel is the crux of the matter and at the same time its problematics. Thus, the metanarrative of diaspora needs to be replaced by the mini narratives in the postmodern sense and each experience of each individual needs to be read in the larger diasporic framework.

*This paper is part of ongoing research for my doctoral thesis.

Works Cited

Anthias, Floyas. "Evaluating 'Diaspora': Beyond Ethnicity?" *Sociology*, vol. 32, no. 3, 1998, pp. 557-80.

Bruneau, Michel. "Diasporas, Transnational Spaces and Communities." *Indian Diasporas and Transnationalism,* ed. Ajay Kumar Sahoo et al. Rawat, 2012, pp. 123-39.

Cohen, Robin. *Global Diasporas: An Introduction*. 1st Indian ed., Routledge, 2010, pp. 17-18.

Hofstede, Geert. *Culture's Consequences: International Differences in Work Related Values.* Sage, 1980.

Medam Alain. Qtd. Lisa Anteby-Yemini and William Berthomière. "Diaspora: A Look Back on a Concept," *Bulletin du Centre de recherché françaisà Jérusalem*, vol. 16, 2005, pp. 262-70.

Reese, Jennifer. "Books in Brief: Fiction; West Is More East" *The New York Times* 25 June, 2000.

Rushdie, Salman. *Imaginary Homelands: Essays and Criticisms 1981-1991*, Penguin Random House, 1992.

Safran, William. *Diasporas in Modern Societies: Myths of Homeland and Return*, Diaspora, vol. 1, no. 1, 1991, pp. 83-99.

_____. "Concepts, Theories, and Challenges of Diaspora: A Panoptic Approach," 2007. www.SISSCO.it>Attivita>ConvegnieIncontridella...>Incontri2007.

Sheffer, proposes a distinction between two categories of diasporas. Sheffer, Gabriel. *Modern Diasporas in International Politics*. Saint Martin Press, 1986.

Sareen, Santosh. "A Home Everywhere: The Consciousness of Diasporic Belonging." *Theorizing and Critiquing Indian Diaspora*, Shodhganga.inflibnet.ac.in/jspui/bitstream/10603/121161/5/05_introductions.pdf.

Syal, Meera. *Life isn't all ha ha hee hee*. 1999. BlackSwan, 2000.

_____. "Meera Syal: 'I didn't want to reach 50 and be full of regrets,'" interview by Jonathan Owen. *Independent,* Sunday 6 May 2012.

The Self and Its Façade: Reflection and Recognition: A Study of Richa Dhawan's *No I Can't Make Round Rotis: Stories of Guts and Grace*

C.R. VISWESWARA RAO
Former Vice-Chancellor, Vikrama Simhapuri Univ., Nellore

No I Can't Make Round Rotis (New Delhi: Prestige Books International, 2021) is the maiden collection from a new face in the Indo-Australian fiction scene, Richa Dhawan. One significant feature of Richa Dhawan's narratives is that they reveal facets of contemporary social reality by exploring the anxieties and enigmas of a female-centred world in an urban environment. The themes that Richa Dhawan touches upon are varied and they range from male hegemony and gender role reversal, the glare of social media and the promptings of the self, the true self and its altruistic façade, disharmony in marriage, gossip and its rebounding effect, superstitious faith and the comedy of errors arising from it, and such other. If "round rotis" symbolize roundedness, most of these characters in the collection find themselves square pegs in a round hole and hanker after roundedness.

In giving her readers a peep into contemporary society and its cultural milieu, mores and concerns where technology has come in but the soul is lost, Richa rethinks her tropes and motifs and reimagines her stories differently. These stories are characterized by economy of setting, concise narrative, and omission of a complex plot. But within the compact space of her narratives Richa can provide twists and turns and reach O'Henry endings. Character is disclosed in action and also through lucid dialogue. Within the limited scope of a short story, Richa Dhawan places her main characters before us in all their abilities and frailties in a manner that assures the reader of her command over voice and setting and her ability to navigate through life's random quirks and cruelties. One objective of the short story writer is that he or she must "link the physical landscape to the mental landscape of the characters," and show the setting through the eyes of a character and through dialogue rather than through a dull and drab narration. That is where the imaginative act lies, which Richa Dhawan displays in abundance in these short stories.

"Nimbu Paani" is a subtle feminist narrative with a difference. It is totally devoid of vehemence or assertion or spokesperson espousal. It takes its title after an exotic drink, a talisman that charms those that Reena comes into contact with. It is a symbol of domesticity, a magical potion that builds up relationships, that brings Reena and Nitya together, and that extracts Nitya's confession, a confession where the issue of crime and punishment is beside the matter. Nitya's confession leads Reena to introspect on her own freedom of choice and her ability to display her creativity so that she can make her husband Vikas's Indian clothing store in a Sidney suburb exude the charm that she can create through her *nimbu paani* and her hidden artistic talent. Now there is another question of moral implication here. Nitya committed a crime, a consequence of gender role reversal and male hegemony. She successfully escaped from the clutches of law by convincing the police that her husband Tarun's was an accidental fall. And she now confesses to Reena, under the spell of *nimbu paani*, that it was she who pushed her husband down the stairs and waited till he bled to death. Why does Reena forgive her? Here is a case of the law versus affinity with womanhood and its urges and insufficiencies. It was Tarun who first tried to push Nitya down the stairs so as perhaps to cause her an abortion, because the arrival of the baby would mean loss of freedom for him, loss of his alpha male status.

Nitya wanted her freedom, her justice. She wanted to be pregnant and her choice and its sanctity made her resort to a counter-offensive. Reena realizes the sanctity behind the counter-offensive and hence the moral implications get crossed out. This short story is a fine exposition of marginality as a site of resistance. It traces, incidentally, the interconnecting patterns that form the substratum of the subalternity of women.

"Follow Me on Instagram" is on a different theme and it is a very relevant, contemporary narrative on addiction to the social media. It is the story of Maya, "moti," "kaali," and "choti," looking like an ugly "panda," dejected, and seeking refuge in death. She bumps at Connaught Place into her former boyfriend who was making a video for Instagram, Amolville. He has a large following on Instagram and he persuades Maya to have a selfie with him, which he posts on Instagram. Very soon, likes and friend requests for Maya start pouring in, such as has never happened to her before. This is a strange and new experience to be under constant internet gaze. Maya now begins to retrospect on the episode of her brief friendship with Nafisa Singh who appropriates for herself the script "Being ugly is beautiful" written by Maya. Lured by the Instagram gaze and the hitherto unavailing attention to her, Maya starts posting pictures of herself in Instagram with such filter adjustments as would help her create a make-believe world for herself, a world in which she slowly starts believing and living, making it pass for the real. Her social media addiction, and the fakery she indulged in for it, make her live rather in this virtual world, leaving aside her real world. When does Maya's mother's wish, "I just want my daughter back," get fulfilled? Not until after her mother's death when the truth dawns on her. Till then, the glare of the social media gripped her in the fear: "you snooze, you lose." In fact, she drew mileage out of her mother's death too until this moment of startling revelation, recognition, peripeteia. She realizes that Tejas, her mother's car driver, addicted to social media, saw Maya's Instagram post informing her followers about her mother's death on his phone book and instantly scribbled a note there while driving: "You are an inspiration, Maya." This momentary distraction from driving led to the accident, to Maya's mother's death. The denouement is like the unfolding of a scene of peripeteia in Greek drama which drives Maya to remorse bringing about an anagnorisis. The de-addiction instantly happens and Maya becomes a vehement advocate of the adverse effects of social media. Maya's message therefore is "New Technology: Handle it with care," a very relevant message to the media-obsessed, tech-savvy society.

"Paradigm Shift" is a different kind of story involving anagnorisis and peripeteia, recognition and reversal. Samanta, successful in her career in a financial consultancy firm adores her mother, her "my angel" figure, selfless and altruistic. Her mother adopted her from an orphanage in Delhi and gave her an elevated social status. Samanta enjoyed parental care and support and her education was especially cared for by her parents. Naturally, therefore, there is a professional award for Samanta in recognition of her work. She has an in-house servant Pinky, an excellent house keeper, towards whom Sam has deep empathy, which Prateek, Sam's lover, recognizes. Mrs. Joseph, Sam's mother, has her assumptions about the servant class in general and Pinky in particular. This story too ends with a sudden revelation and a feeling of culpability that marks a possible chastening. To her consternation Mrs. Joseph learns from Pinky that she too came from the same orphanage from which Sam was adopted. In fact, her father, a cancer patient, had appealed to Mrs. Joseph to adopt his daughter but she preferred Sam because what mattered was looks, and the humanitarian concern that ought to have been shown to Pinky took the back seat. Pinky's large, ugly birthmark on her face marks her undoing, the nipping in the bud of a possible fairy tale. But Sam's empathy, already hinted at in the story, makes her "adopt" Pinky as it were as her orphanage sister. When Mrs. Joseph confesses that she picked Sam over Pinky with an ugly birthmark, she stands, of her own admission before Sam, culpable for her lack of humanitarian concern.

"Gossip Queen" drives home the message that "knowledge is power when knowledge is right." It is a satire on addiction to WhatsApp and on the penchant for gossip and vandalizing. Seema, the receptionist at a medical centre in Delhi, loves gossip and her obsession with Facebook and Instagram centre her activity round gathering tidbits, casually and with malice towards none. She habitually spreads conjectures about the lives of people around and indulges in vituperation in her daily chat. She never realizes the damage it may cause to people whose personal lives she targets. There is a dramatic turn to her story when Seema falls in a subtle trap laid for her by Dr. Alok, Dr. Nicky and Dr. Madhu who get to know about the rumours about them she has deliberately spread. The doctor trio works out a happy denouement by subtly turning the tables against her to teach her a moral lesson.

"Happily Married" is a tale of murder with a difference. Its twists and turns show the obese Shreya, a kindergarten teacher, finding her soulmate in Karan, a loving husband whom she kills. Her version of why she killed him is vividly dramatized through the interrogation Kavita conducts. During the interrogation Kavita finds Shreya evasive in her replies, for there is a truth behind the evasion Shreya feels uneasy about revealing. From an interrogator's point of view, the motive, when it is scanty, leads to an inevitable conviction. But Shreya feels that prison is less of a humiliation than disclosing the truth. Shreya recounts how after her marriage the truth slowly dawns on her that she was in a "matrimonial cage" and that Karan was a gay in relationship with Sunil. Shreya killed him not because he was gay but because he put on the appearance of a saviour and preyed on her because she was fat and no one would be after her. She was an object which he possessed and his parents' homophobia made him behave the way he did, so possessively. But Shreya's mother gives the final twist to the plot when she reveals that Shreya was indeed a bisexual who couldn't find a partner in a man. The story explores psychological angles of misfits in marriage.

"The Truth of a Myth" centres round custom-ridden Indian society where compatibility between the horoscopes is a must for an arranged marriage to happen. Where there is no agreement, ludicrous appeasement rituals are suggested, and Sudha superstitiously believes that these rituals countenance astrological obstacles to a marriage. When it comes to her second son Anil who is bent on marrying the girl of his choice, Sudha protests and resists but learns to her consternation from her husband that their own marriage was made possible by bribing the elder *panditji* to pronounce compatibility where it did not astrologically exist. But they have been a happy couple enjoying their longevity. This revelation, backed up by other revelations that disprove astrology, makes Sudha see through the myth of the reality she has so far believed in due to her faith in superstition.

"Superwoman" is a different kind of story that envisages an afterlife to Diya, the rape victim who now turns a saviour, a "superwoman messiah" who sees and hears vulnerable women so as to help them walk out of their cocoons. The story ends with the suggestion that objectification of women may continue but women are emboldened to reach the zero-tolerance level. In its narrative patterning "Superwoman" seems to follow Helene Cixous's idea that woman must write her *self.* It is a fine story that in a sense leads to an excavation of the archaeology of women's suffering from which the rhetoric of rebellion and rupture arise.

"The End of Carpe Diem: An epistle to my children" is an address in epistolary form to be read ten years later. It is on the corona virus and the destabilization it has caused in lives, the speculations and defamation it has given rise to, the social messaging sites that have become busy spreading fake news, and what our resolve should be for the future: whether to live a carpe diem kind of existence or look beyond for the return of the old normal and its spirit of mutuality. It reminds us of Robert Frost's poem "Carpe Diem" which deserves to be quoted:

> The present is

too much for the senses,
Too crowding, too confusing-
Too present to imagine.

Richa Dhawan portrays the corona virus as a tragedy worse than *Hamlet*. The corona virus's ramifications like Work from Home (WFH) and Home-Based Learning (HBL) and the "parenting battles" they have caused are surely a matter for retrospection years later when the dust settles down. But what is significant about this epistle is that it is interlaced with the story of Chandni, the street dog, and is placed in a frame that refers to Yann Martel's *Life of Pi*, a Canadian philosophical novel that explores a story of self-actualization through the tracing of a traumatic experience of shipwreck and survival on a life boat in the Pacific Ocean with a Bengali Tiger, questioning as it were the nature of reality and how it is perceived and told, like Chandni's own tale of fortitude.

Richa Dhawan's short stories help us reflect on snapshots of life that sometimes delineate moments glimpsed in passing. These short stories concentrate on a single effect conveyed in a few significant episodes. They are characterized by economy of setting, concise narrative, and the omission of a complex plot. Character is disclosed in action and dramatic encounter. These stories are centred round women but do not espouse an altogether feminist standpoint in spite of the subtle critique of Indian marriages that they contain. With their occasional critical analyses of gender roles, the short stories are lucid, tender, witty, and reflective. The scene, setting and the experience depicted are Indian but they have a broad universal appeal in terms of the paradigms of experience they place before us. Some of the short stories have an epiphanic ending, in the sense of a sudden revelation or insight, which inspires the character resulting in a change of outlook. Every story is different, incongruous with the rest, and yet they all come together like an exquisite exposition of human character. It is a collection that seeks to anchor our generation down with its esoteric lifestyles and its mundane musings.

Negotiating Cultural Spaces in Recent Travel Writings on India

PRADEEP TRIKHA
M.L.S. University, Udaipur

> We cannot separate literature and art from other kinds of social practice in such a way as to make them subject to quite special and distinct laws.
>
> Raymond Williams
>
> There is no foreign land; it is only the traveller that is foreign.
>
> Robert Louis Stevenson

Literature is the mirror held towards social and political milieu of its times. The paper proposes to look into cultural spaces in two non-fictional texts; both are travelogues by two prominent voices in John Zubrzycki and William Dalrymple. Travel writing often reveals the history of the explored land through the cultural lens of the traveller. A well-acclaimed travel critic Mary Campell has elaborated on the significant concerns of the traveller, while encountering a foreign culture: "It, therefore, represents not only the changing times but also the intra-cultural transformations along with the socio-political and demographic changes, that happened in a [society] with a long history" (53). The paper attempts to analyze how the writers under consideration seem to be genuinely in love with India's past and the present. Zubrzycki, an Australian, former diplomat and journalist, was so besotted by the country that he came out with his third book *The Empire of Enchantment: The Story of Indian Magic* which is a compendium of India's magic history, its Indian edition is known as *Jadoowallahs, Jugglers and Jinns*. However, unlike Zubrzycki,

Dalrymple, from Britain takes an incisive look into the enthralling and enigmatic features of the ancient modern city of Delhi in his *City of Djinns: A Year in Delhi*. For the first time, he visited Delhi when he was seventeen to work and serve in Mother Teresa's old age home as a volunteer. Nevertheless, seven years later he came as a tourist and stayed back. Steve Clark, in an "Introduction" to *Asian Crossings*, points out: "the academic study of travel writing coincides fairly precisely with the emergence of postcolonial studies, for which the genre serves as a convenient paradigm of cross-cultural encounter, inevitably inscribed with the dynamics of power relations between centre and periphery. Thus, the study of travelogue enlarges the traditional literary canon and challenges any residual ideal of the classic text as aesthetically self-contained and autonomous." (12)

Foucault emphasizes 'space as the site of relations' (14) and so is cultural space that is a site of cultural relations or at times of cultural materialism. Throughout history, magic has occupied a special place on the margins of society. It defines the contours of experiences that are in some way, exceptional or outside normal and every day. To some extent, this denigrated position echoes the location of religion and even science. Foucault contends that space is fundamental in any form of communal life; space is produced socially and culturally, and various spaces coexist within the same physical space.

Each physical space has cultural nuances in this sense, theories of new criticism and cultural materialism mark the return to history in literary criticism. Cultural materialists tend to read the text as the material products of the specific historical conditions. Sumanta Banerjee, in her essay "The Mysterious Alien: Indian Street Jugglers in Victorian London," points out that "during the urbanization process in London the masses were imported from Asian and African underclass as sailors, servants and nannies. Once their utility was over they were dismissed and left on tenterhooks to fend for themselves, these Indian immigrants underclass turned to skills in entertainments like jugglery and similar ones, and occupied important space in the urban landscape of the 19th century England." (61)

According to John Storey, culture refers to the "shared meanings we make and encounter in our everyday lives . . . the practices and processes of making meanings with and from the 'texts' we encounter in our everyday lives" (221). The acclaimed theorist, Raymond Williams, defines culture as "ordinary and as a way of life" (23). He gives three different definitions of culture: the lived culture, the recorded culture, the period culture and culture of the selective tradition. Cultural Studies is a field that seeks to find how culture functions in the modern world, cultural productions work, and the formation of cultural identities. Travel writing is an exciting medium to translate culture, as the writer travels, it makes observations and translates the observations based on real experiences verbally through the travelogue. The firmament of travel writing has gained popularity and wide acceptance over time. The traveller uses the work as a mouthpiece to take the readers to new destinations and exposes that place's culture in a detailed manner through vivid descriptions. Travelogues serve as a bridge between two cultural identities; it would be compelling and thought-provoking to take up a travelogue and interrogate the various problems in translating cultural nuances of the travelled country.

II

In 1828 William Hazlitt in his essay the "Indian Jugglers" described a stunning performance by an Indian juggler and praised his "skill surmounting difficulty and beauty triumphing over skill." The present paper tries to analyze the cultural spaces as portrayed in the *Empires of Enchantment*. It explores how the power relations existing in society create space that formulates the citizens' identity and subjectivity. As social beings, we feel entertained with space that reflects the ideology, power politics, and so forth of the institutions. Similarly, cultural materialism privileges power relationships as the most important context for interpreting the text. Zubrzycki's book puts on record several casts of characters like Ramo Samee (possibly corrupted form of Rama Swamy) who became a household name in 1800s England for his juggling and sword swallowing, as Tishani Doshi points out in her article, "John Zubrzycky's new book looks at magic in India," "skills to Ganapati Chakraborty who began as a stuntman in the Great Bengal Circus" who performed 'illusion of a box.' Zubrzycky further explains that ancient India was a fun place for *Jaadu*-miracle contests between Sufis and Yogis Buddhists and Jains battling it out with spell incantations; warrior God Indra, the first great magician, casting his *indra jaal.* There are times when Zubrzycki uses 'magic' and 'witchcraft' as interchangeable terms. Zubrzycki is an effusive traveller, for whom magic is an irresistible topic; he looks into encounters between the East and West and the considerable influence that Indian enchantment has had on the rest of the world. For him different kinds of magic in India for centuries have been blurring the boundaries between mythology, ritual, religion and performance, covering the gambit from snake charmers, rope dancers, astrologers and contour contortionists and underpinned by the concept of *maya.* Many of the magicians were from marginalized communities and illiterate.

Zubrzycki narrates Emperor Jahangir's enchantment by a troupe of Bengali jugglers as revealed through his memoirs, and several foreign travellers—Megasthenes, ambassador at the court of Chandragupta Maurya, Marco Polo, Ibn Battuta mesmerized with the magic tricks of Indian jugglers. In the historical times, magicians from India moved across trade routes of ancient Rome, Tang dynasty of China and the Baghdad Caliphate. Interestingly, in a burial chamber in Egypt, 2500 BC has a pictorial depiction of two men performing the cups and balls tricks.

III

Dalrymple makes insightful observations about Delhi's present as well as past history. *City of Djinns* is the result of

Dalrymple's research and stay in the historic city of Delhi. When he landed up in this city, he was a newly married young man accompanied by his wife, Olivia Fraser.

Huma Yakub, in her article, "William Dalrymple's *City of Djinns* and the Hegemonic Strategies of Travel Writing" infers, "In the very prologue to the book, Dalrymple celebrates the unique character of this city—the quality of rising back to life from its ashes like a phoenix. Delhi has been visualized as a city that refuses to annihilate and redefines itself after each destruction phase. Dalrymple makes use of motifs of decadence and ruin in order to describe Delhi. *City of Djinns* moves freely from the present to the past and from personal experiences to historical, cultural and mythical." (94)

The prologue gives an idea of coming and provides the reader with information regarding the book's title. Dalrymple recounts his meeting with the Sufi Pir Sadr-ud-Din who calls Delhi the *City of Djinns* and it is because of the love of the djinns for this city it can never be deserted. The book is, in fact, a backward journey in the history and culture of Delhi—a journey into the Orient with tales of Sufis and Djinns, decadent emperors with their harems and courtesans; beautiful Asian women and fights of partridges. For the writer, Delhi is a land of heat and dust, a land improved and civilized by the British Raj. Dalrymple describes it as a city of contradictions and once he establishes his fascination and love for the same he gets the authority to unfold the city like an Orientalist: "Delhi, it seemed at first, was full of riches and horrors: it was a labyrinth, a city of palaces, an open gutter, filtered light through a filigree lattice, a landscape of domes, anarchy, a press of people, a choke of fumes, a whiff of spices" (India—Gavin Thomas Travel. https://gavinthomas.wordpress.com/tag/india/). In his book on Delhi, William Dalrymple points out that there are many Delhis and they cannot be decoded in linearity; therefore, he moved through the time and space looking and holding in circles and parabolas of the past and present. (79)

He begins his narrative from Nizamuddin, then moves to the years of partition and post-independence, then traces New Delhi's emergence in the early 20th century and then more in-depth into the twilight period, the years from Nadir Shah depredation of 1739 to 1857 Mutiny. With curiosity, he delves into the historical space. Like Foucault, he believes that space produces social and cultural spaces which coexist within the same physical space. In Delhi, it is a fact that power relations have always created a space that goes beyond all the concepts regarding normalcy.

In his article Zubrzycky points out a fascinating historical record, "on the 7th November 1889, an unusual procession marched down the main street of Melbourne" (https://www.livehistory-india.com) witnessed by many the troupe of Indian magicians wearing turbans and brightly coloured robes accompanied by nautch girls made their way to the city court demanding their wages and passage home. For historians, it is jugglers' mutiny.

Today, social historians should not rush to discover patriotism in Britain's performances; their acts of the display were motivated by different impulses. Altogether they were impelled on words by powerful socio-economic forces that were shaping the organization of Victorian London. They were not fully aware of the historic role that they were playing. These forgotten Indian immigrants act as a catalyst in recasting the 18th and 19th century London as a Cosmopolitan city, and they are around reconstruction as urban cities. Western reception of Indian magic was also influenced by the prevailing racial prejudice in that period. The performances of magic became an ideological battlefield during the colonial era driven by both professional rivalry and feelings of racial superiority; European magicians tried to discredit Indian magic and magicians. The Indians responded by appropriating their Western counterparts' techniques and gimmicks to beat them at their own game.

Dalrymple like Zubrzycky manages to move from the present to the past and back, at times he even adds a thrilling element, for example, when he discovers *Tykhana* beneath Fraser's mansion. His love's labour for Delhi is not lost.

Understanding the ambiguous and paradoxical role of travel and celebrity culture, Robert Clarke observes: "Modern Western travel culture, like a celebrity, it could be said, has played a dubious role in the development of capitalist democratic cultures, as a force and symbol of enfranchisement and liberation, on the one hand, and equally of containment and exploitation, on the other. In recent scholarship, travel has been figured either as oppressive and colonizing, or as a force for disruption, Hybridity and liberation" (145). This ambiguity and duality also underline *City of Djinns* and Dalrymple himself; as a celebrity travel writer. By penning this book, Dalrymple exhibits his fascination for India and mainly for Delhi, but at the same time, the book betrays his hegemonic colonial strategies.

On the other hand, getting back to Zubrzycki's book, some other magic centres around Lucknow, Calcutta and Madras had great attraction not only for the Indians but also for their colonial masters. Later a ban was imposed on magicians travelling to perform in the world exhibitions that were a rage in the 1900s many flouted the law by skipping from Madras to Ceylon and onwards leading to a larger question: vanishing act of magic itself. There, are, of course, successful magicians working in India like P.C. Sorcar Jr. and his daughter Maneka whose shows sell out wherever they go, but anti-beggary laws and fewer public spaces mean that street magic is disappearing. Though there is hardly any hope for its revival, Zubrzycki emphasizes the importance of enchantment in our lives.

The 19th century was perhaps the most eventful period for magicians. In the 1880s, a company of 'Cabul Jugglers and East Indian Magicians accompanied Afghan Museum, and Oriental Curiosity Bazaar' visited Australia. The 'Museum of Indian Curiosities' opened in Adelaide in June 1889; the curiosities included five-legged cow, weapons, musical instruments, shoes, trays, inlaid with marble work and other similar objects. The performers included Paine Pindarrum, 'a juggler of higher-order' who demonstrated the cups and balls trick, produced fire from his mouth and spat out dozens of two inches long nails and Galip Sahab, who executed 'the Basket Trick' with a young girl named Giddy. Within a few weeks of their arrival in Melbourne, however, police were called to investigate mistreatment allegations.

Magic, fantasy, *mayajaal* and *indrajaal* are no longer the past of extraordinary memory, but it is indeed an enthralling treasure which is now becoming history and cultural inheritance. Zubrzycki feels that the *jaduwallahs*, the jugglers, the *kathputli-walas*, hypnotists, conjurors and street performers live in penury, only very few get an opportunity to become cultural emissaries to perform at international cultural exchange program.

Indeed, in one of the editions, the cover shows a snake charmer playing his pipe lying on a bed of nails. During the 1950s P.C. Sorcar billed himself as 'The World's Greatest Magician' and 'Maharaja of Magic' made optimum use of available media to advertise his magic tricks. Similarly, Gogia Pasha the world-renowned Egyptian Master of Magic, plied his trade in Australia. His tricks included 'X-ray Eyes' and 'Basket of Death.'

IV

On the basis of preceding analysis, the socio-cultural space structures our understanding of ourselves and the others around us. It is not a neutral space at all. Andrzej Zielenice, a cultural theorist in his essay, 'Ideology and Ideological State Apparatuses,' points out: "The social construction of space is both historically and socially contingent and dependent on the operation of relation and process of power and knowledge" (121). As social beings, the lives of magicians reflect the ideology, power, politics and so on of the institution existing within it. A conquest of social relations leads to a democratic dominance of unique relations and vice versa. *The Empire of Enchantment* can be considered materialist text because Zubrzycki probes into the ideology in material form institutions like museums and exhibitions and royal courts. He highlights that cultural space pursued and persistently created by South Asia's magicians is a field of much ideological contest and contradiction that no cultural artefact or practice is outside the political sphere or space. The power relations create a space which goes beyond all concepts regarding normalcy.

According to Bernard Mc Grane, "To travel is to see—travel is essentially a way of seeing, a mode of seeing: it is grounded in the eye, in our visual capacity" (116). As suggested by Giorgia Alù and Sarah Patricia Hill, in their article, "The travelling eye: reading the visual in travel narratives," historically, it is above all those "distant places, landscapes, foreign people, animals, and objects seem to gain consistency." The gaze is then transferred into the text, whether in written or in visual form. In travel writing, views and gazes express a narrative space from which narrator and reader scrutinize, judge and categorize the varied cultures and societies they explore through writing and reading. Illustrations, in particular, come to play a central role in the perception of places and people. For centuries, sketches, watercolours, engravings, lithographs, photography, film, and digital media have framed and recorded every aspect of our movements and experiences of dislocation. They have played a key role in supporting the traveller observer's claims of reliability and truthfulness and need "to conjure up the appearances of something absent" (Berger, 10). In travel writings and related texts, visual images mark an experience as bona fide; they confirm that objects, signs and elements (for example, buildings, places, customs and physical features of natives) have been seen. Simultaneously, any form of visual representation is often less realistic than it seems; it distorts rather than reflects social reality. Paul Burke suggests that the process of distortion is itself evidence of specific phenomena: "mentalities, ideologies and identities. In other words, pictures testify to the mental and metaphorical 'image' of the Self and/ or of the other." (30-31)

Dalrymple also effectively establishes the western hegemony by establishing the inherent differences between the English West and the Indian East; be it in architecture, governance, culture, behaviour and moral codes. Following Western Orientalist tradition, Dalrymple without being directly judgmental portrays Mughal rulers as promiscuous, cruel and incestuous. Repeated references have been made in the travelogue; through anecdotes and quoting 'fanciful speculations' by Western travellers like Manucci and Bernier regarding Shah Jehan's fondness for her eldest daughter Jahanara Begum that the great Mughal emperor nurtured an incestuous desire for her. Many contemporary writers comment on Shah Jehan's legendary appetites: the Emperor's lust for his daughter Jahanara, his penchant for seducing the wives of his generals and relations, and the numbers of courtesans invited into the palace to quench the monarch's thirst when his expansive harem proved insufficient (231). Fluctuating between the historical past and the present of Delhi, Dalrymple describes his various visits to the shrine of Sufi Saint Nizamuddin Aulia and the Jama Masjid on the occasion of *Eid namaz*. Dr. Jaffery, a resident of Old Delhi, is his guide during most of these explorations. Old Delhi from the rooftop gives him space to talk about kite fliers and pigeon fliers (*kabooter baaz*)—a complete picture of the Orient from the western eye. Moving further back into the history of Delhi, the author takes his readers for a journey into 14th century when the Moroccan traveller Ibn Batuta arrived in Delhi and got appointed to the post of Qazi by Sultan Muhammad-bin-Tughlaq. Dalrymple closes his book by devoting only a few pages to the ancient history of Delhi, and this is where he brings the great Hindu epic *Mahabharata* into focus. In the bygone era Delhi was known as the Indraprastha—the significant capital of the Pandavas that the author calls as 'the Indian Troy' (323), was unparalleled in its grandeur and was termed 'a new heaven' by Vyasa. Thus, it would not be out of place to suggest that both the texts have redemptive significance for the writer and the reader. Julia Cohen and Paul

Smethurst, in an "Introduction" to their seminal work *New Directions in Travel Writing Studies*, ardently point out:

> The impetus for travel writing studies as a discipline itself came in the 1980s when a counter-traditional wave swept through the humanities. In literary studies, interest began to turn from the canon to 'minor texts,' alternative voices and *petits récits* in a war against grand narratives. As Leavisite notions of a 'great tradition' were deconstructed by strategies of 'writing back' and new localisms, a much wider range of texts were made available for scrutiny. Travel writing then emerged from the margins as a significant resource. When the 'theory' revolution took hold in the late 1980s, travel writing proved especially adaptable and responsive to the application of cross-cultural, postcolonial, gender and globalization studies. Cultural historians, geographers and those working in literary studies found in travel writing an endless supply of texts reaching back into antiquity, and across all cultures. Travel writing achieved further prominence in the post-theory critical consciousness from the spatial/ geopolitical turn in the humanities, which took its lead from French theorists, Michel de Certeau, Gilles Deleuze and Felix Guattari, Henri Lefebvre and Michel Foucault. 'Travel' would henceforth provide a rich source of metaphor in theory-based critical practice. Indeed, it supplied much of the lexicon: displacement, (re-)location, (de-)territorialization, mapping, topology, boundaries, space, place, mobility and so on. While this lexicon retains literal currency in travel writing, in critical practice it is almost always used figuratively with terms like 'space' and 'mapping' being overused to the point of cliché. The seductive metaphoricity of these terms is by no means unproblematic when theory is turned back onto travel writing, where it potentially confuses the source with the target of the metaphor. The tendency to aestheticize and universalize the emancipatory potential of travel-related metaphors in critical practice is understandable and well-documented. This is a tendency we need to guard against if we are to avoid a postmodern mire of co-extensive textuality, the loss of referential worlds and a weakened sense of reality" (9-10)

V

The texts taken up for discussion concede to the metaphorical and enfranchise and enlarge the reader's world view. Dalrymple and Zubrzycki suggest that magic and mystery retain a kind of nostalgia in the current situation, which has become recognized as a form of Orientalism. The rise of Street magic demonstrates the 'margins' in which audiences are willing to suspend their disbelief regarding magic have shifted from the distant peripheries of the empire to the boundaries of domestic society, in subcultures and subversion. In magic, the new Orientalism revolves around Brooklyn and Bradford. Meanwhile, Asia, especially East Asia, has become enwrapped in a new kind of Orientalist discourse that we might call it techno-Orientalism because now technologies have taken over several things in everyday life that resemble magic. As a troupe in performance culture, contemporary Asia casts a more natural and powerful spell at technology trade shows than the magician's stage. Orientalism is a device of stage magic that now resides in nostalgia, which of course has a magic of its own.

Works Cited

Alù, Giorgia and Sarah Patricia Hill (2018). "The travelling eye: reading the visual in travel narratives," www.tandfonline.com/doi/ pdf

Banerjee, Sumanta (2011). 'The Mysterious Alien: Indian Street Jugglers in Victorian London," *Economic and Political Weekly*, 46: 14 (April 2-8).

Berger, John (1972). *Ways of Seeing*. London: Penguin.

Burke, Paul (2001). *Eyewitnessing: The Use of Images as Historical Evidence*, London: Reaktion Books.

Campbell. Mary (2002), in Peter Hulme and Tim Young, ed., *The Cambridge Companion to Travel Writing*. Cambridge: Cambridge University Press.

Clarke, Robert (2009). "Travel and Celebrity Culture: An Introduction." *Travel and Celebrity Culture, Postcolonial Studies*, 12: 2.

Clark, Steve (2008), in Steve Clark and Paul Smethurst, ed., *Asian Crossings: Travel Writing on China, Japan and Southeast Asia*. Hong Kong University Press.

Cohen, Julia and Paul Smethurst (2015). *New Directions in Travel Writing Studies*. Palgrave Macmillan.

Dalrymple, William (1993). *City of Djinns: A Year in Delhi*, New Delhi: Bloomsbury.

Doshi, Tishani (2018). "John Zubrzycki's new book looks at magic in India." https://www.thehindu.com/life-and-style/john-zubrzyckis-new-book-looks-at-magic-in-india

Foucault, M. (2008). "Of Other Spaces," in M. Dehaene and L. De Cauter, ed., *Heterotopias and the City: Public Space in a Post Civil Society*, Oxon: Routledge.

Hazlitt, William, "The Indian Jugglers," *Table Talk*, 1828, http://www.juggling.org/papers/hazlitt

Mc Grane, Bernard (1989). *Beyond Anthropology: Society and the Other*, New York: Columbia University Press.

Stevenson, R.L. (1883). *Treasure Island*, Edinburgh: Chatto & Windus.

Storey, John (2007). *Cultural Theory and Popular Culture: An Introduction*, University of Sunderland.

William, Raymond (1977). *Marxism and Literature*. Oxford Univ. P.

Ykub, Huma (2014). "William Dalrymple's *City of Djinns* and the Hegemonic Strategies of Travel Writing," *International Journal of English and Literature*, 4: 1.

Zieleniec, Andrzej (2007). *Space and Social Theory*, London: Sage.

Zubrzycki, John (2018). The 'Jugglers' Mutiny' https://www.livehistoryindia.com/cover-story/2018/06/17/the-jugglers-mutiny

_____ (2018). *Jadoowallahs, Jugglers and Jinns: A Magical History of India*, Picador India.

Travel, Gender, Norms: A Study of Dervla Murphy's *Full Tilt: Ireland to India with a Bicycle*

NEELAM YADAV
Delhi College of Arts and Commerce, University of Delhi

> The essence of adventure lies in taking risks and exploring the unknown, so it is hardly surprising to find that early travel accounts tended for the most part to be written by men, who moved more freely in the public sphere.[1]

> Historically, the discourse of absence is carried on by the Woman: Woman is sedentary, Man hunts, journeys; Woman is faithful (she waits), man is fickle (he sails away, he cruises).[2]

The above quotes sum up the deep-rooted 'patriarchal ideology of separate spheres' occupied by male and female traveller/ travel writers and also the skewed attitude of scholars towards them. When we talk about women and travel writing, two basic interpretations come to our mind. First, it conveys the idea of women as represented in travel writings and second, women as travel writers. Women in travel writings are always represented as the ignored, stereotypical 'silent woman' or the passive companion, who has been to distant land but only as a daughter, a wife or a mother of the male traveller. "Even though women have shared the experiences of travel with men, much of the critical attention to travel has focused on the male traveller or a male paradigm of travel," states Susan Roberson.[3] In the past, the idea of travel has always been associated with men; man has been the central subject of all travel accounts written since time immemorial. But when women travellers become travel writers, there was an illusionary shift in the status of woman from a personal/ private to public domain. But, even after this deceiving upheaval of the status, works of female writers were either subsumed by male writers or completely neglected by critics and readers alike. Though many feminist/female scholars like Sara Mills, Susan Bassnett, and Shirley Foster question the biased attitude male scholars have towards women traveller/ travel writers, hardly any male scholar has paid any critical attention to female travel writers. This skewed mentality of male critics is evident in the works of Paul Fussel, Denis Porter, and Peter Hulme who have delineated women writers as a 'non-existent gender'[4] in the genre of travel writing. The reason for this biased treatment is that various assumptions and presumptions are associated with women traveller/ travel writers; as a result, the role and contribution of women as travellers and as travel writers suffer conventional suppression. These assumptions, which are discussed in detail later in this paper have become myths. Hence, several 'myths' are in play when women travel writings are read and analyzed, which by and large has resulted in the gendering of the whole genre of travel and travel writing.

The purpose of this paper is not to find out why women were not allowed to travel and give voice to their experiences of travelling, if they travel at all, but the focus of this paper is on the premise that almost all the pre-conceived notions and the 'received wisdom'[5] about the gendering of travel, to a very great extent, is a myth. The paper also tries to contest the concept of gendering of travel by elucidating legendary Irish travel writer, Dervla Murphy's debut travel work, *Full Tilt: Ireland to India with a Bicycle.*

'Women are not sufficiently concerned either with travel or with writing itself' opines Paul Fussell (98). Dervla Murphy's *Full Tilt* pensively challenges this norm. She is one such travel writer who has travelled almost half the world and has authored more than 20 travel books based on her incredible journeys to myriad countries. Since her early childhood, travelling and writing were her two passions. This travelogue recounts her incredible travelling for six months on a bicycle, named 'Roz,' across Europe and through Persia, Afghanistan, Pakistan into India, during 'the coldest winter in eighty years.'[6] For almost six months she travelled to those remote places where travelling by men is considered to be perilous. I quote the words of a reviewer, Clifford Graves (as critics and scholars usually find it demeaning to analyze woman travel writer) who blurted out that he couldn't believe that any 'woman' can even dream of travelling to the countries Ms. Murphy journeyed, that too, alone: "I had not counted on a young *woman—repeat, woman*—who brought off the most difficult part of such a journey, alone and unaided."[7] *Full Tilt* recounts tale of Dervla's courage and conviction, self-determination and self-reliance while bicycling across the prohibited/ restricted landscape.

In most of the male scholars' work on travel writing like that of Carl Thompson, Peter Hulme, Eric Newby, it has been deliberately informed that since centuries only a small number of women have got opportunity to travel and only a fraction of the travelled women pen down their experiences and have become travel writers. By deconstructing the history of travel literature, it has been found that myriad literature by women travel writers is lying unearthed and sometimes available under distinct sub-genres like diary writing, autobiography, letter writing, memoir etc., which are not included in the genre of travel literature, as it was the misapprehension, that those were not intended for publication and therefore, inferior in quality. However, history (history of settlers, migration, diaspora, partition) records that in every period and at every level of society, women have travelled as housewives, settlers, migrants, missionaries, scholars, adventurers, explorers, and have also recorded their experiences of travelling in literary writings. But, due to gendering of travel, their works have gone unrecorded and unaccounted for. But, there were still some distinguished women travellers/travel writers like Isabella Bird, Mary

Kingsley, Lady Mary Montagau, Margery Kempe, Florence Nightingale, to name a few, whose works got circulated/published in their lifetime and made them 'exceptional women' of their time.[8] *Maiden Voyages: Writings of Women Travellers* by Mary Morris, *Great Women Travel Writers: From 1750 to the Present* edited by Alba Amoia, *Ladies on the Loose, Women's Travel Literature from Travellers' Tales, The Best Women's Travel Writing, Blessings of a Good, The Thick Skirt* and *Spinsters Abroad*, to name a few, are some of the collections which record travel experiences of those women travellers who refused to conform to the social norms of the day, travelled across the world and got their experiences published.

One more preconceived notion related to the gendering of travel is that virtually all early (especially before 19th century) women travel writings were in the form of letters, diary entries, memoirs or sketches as these genre of literature were considered to be less risky and less literary and weren't written with any intention of publication. It is also believed that diary writing offers "woman the possibility of laying claim to writing while allaying the anxieties of actual publication" as claimed by an anthologist, Jane Robinson.[9] However, time and again, the notion of publication has been questioned and contested by scholars and critics differently. It has been misrepresented that women travellers intend to write for the amusement of a private circle of relatives and friends rather for publication, whereas, says Susan Bassnett in *Cambridge Companion to Travel Writing,'* male writers have had publication in mind from the outset.' (226) But, Susan Roberson opines that when it comes to publication, class rather than gender plays a more important role. She cites examples of upper-class American women travel writers to substantiate her argument, "American women's travel writing divides along class lines, with more educated women like Harriet Beecher Stowe, Edith Wharton, and Margaret Fuller writing professionally for publication, while other women write primarily for themselves or family, publication being only an incidental concern" (216). But Dervla Murphy has no such fear of publication, except for her autobiography, *Wheels within Wheels*, which needed a little persuasion from her publishers,[10] rest of her works were written with publication in mind from the very onset. Although she has written all her works in the diary form, they are in no sense an aspect inferior in quality. She was a persistent and meticulous diarist. In the course of her journeying, she used to pen down everything at the end of each day, sometimes intensely subjective, other days recounting just the landscape travelled and people she met on the way, but always truthful and correct, vivid and valuable.

Now, I move on to discuss some other preconceived notions, prejudices and norms which always pervade in the mind of readers and scholars while reading the works of women travel writers. Women travel writings, as considered by many male scholars (Foucault, in particular), are in many sense, autobiographical and 'confessional.'[11] It is also believed that female travellers write more about their 'self' than about the place and the people they visit. If narratives by male travellers are categorized as objective, truthful, factual and unemotional; feminine narratives are classified as personal, domestic, fictional and emotional. While reading Murphy's not only *Full Tilt*, but other works like *Between River and Sea, Through Serbia by Accident, On a Shoestring to Coorg, In Ethiopia with a Mule,* to name a few, one will see that nowhere Murphy has sacrificed accuracy for the sake of making narrative more alluring and fascinating. She confesses in *Full Tilt*, "The temptation to make myself sound more learned than I am, by gleaning facts and figures from an encyclopaedia and inserting them in appropriate places, has been resisted."[12] Her experiences of travelling in these countries were based on factual details (which is supposed to be a male forte of writing)—historically, ethnographically and geographically. She believes that travel writers of all time should focus on giving factual data and details so that historiographers and geographers of the coming time could rely on those descriptions as facts. To make her text more factual and reliable source of information, Dervla has attached a couple of maps and illustrations. A list of requisites she carried with onto her journey to India is also attached at the end of the book. Her narrative provides descriptive information of the places, people and scenic beauty in a gender-neutral way. She focuses more on the place and its people, rest, she says, is 'inessential.'

Critics like Jeanne Denys and B. Norwick accused female narratives of 'exaggeration' and 'falsifications of events.'[13] While analyzing critical works on women travel writing, I have noted that most of the times women writers face a dilemmatic situation. If they maintain the status of being feminine and 'lady-like,' their works are judged as inconsequential and inferior, and if they question and contest the discourses of femininity and delineate their experiences in astonishing voyager type narratives, their work is accused for the 'falsification of events.' So for women travel writers it is always a 'no-win' situation. But Dervla isn't affected by any such categorization. Martina McGlynn and Garret Daly describe Dervla "fiercely independent," and a spirited adventurer, who travels like 'a passionate nomad,' and without carrying a 'feminine status of sophistication.'[14] It was the same reason that while journeying abroad, Dervla was often considered a man, "A white woman riding a bicycle alone across the breadth of a country like, say, Afghanistan, was completely unheard of; so much so, that many people assumed she was a man."[15] During one of her trips to Cameroon with her daughter Rachel, Dervla was frequently mistaken for Rachel's husband. But this confusion over gender identity opens up another discourse of discussion, i.e. cross-dressing while travelling, which I will not discuss here in detail as it needs at least three thousand more words to convey my views. But for Dervla, dressing is just a necessity to cover her body, "One of the joys of the expedition was getting away from dress with its worries as distinguished from mere clothes,"[16] says Murphy riding Roz in her tattered trousers.

Like clothes, gender is just a fact of life. While answering the question regarding her identity in terms of gender, she answers very succinctly, 'gender is, just there, you're not focusing on it. It's just how you are, you're a woman, that's it."[17] Dervla controls her own discourse. She never lets her gender to constrain her views and thought. For her gender is just one of the many factors which make you what you are. Hence, the geographically authentic account of the terrain travelled, her comments on the political issues of the country she was in, self-defence techniques/weapons used by her during the time of crisis, all these and many more circumstances and situations themselves contest the over-generalized statement that Jane Robinson posed in her *Wayward Women*: 'men's travel account is to do with What and Where, and woman's with How and Why?'[18]

An image is formed by the scholars and male writers that women travellers believe in familiarization or domestication of the unfamiliar while male travellers move beyond any such constraints. However, it is also presumed that even when a woman travels away from home, she tries to make the place more like home. The reason for that is being the conventional image of a woman as 'sessile,' 'angel of the house,' and as someone who's always happy to be at home. For Dervla Murphy, travelling is liberating, and self-seeking. Apart from incessant references to availability, scarcity and type of food, she didn't refer much to her personal habits and life. For the same reasons of familiarizing distant as home, she hates technology. Once in an interview she confesses how much she dislikes technology. She argues that if by "mere pressing the buttons of your mobile phone, you are with your folks back home, 'then why bother leaving home?"'[19]

It is no more than a cliche that women traditions of writing are self-evidently different from their male counterparts. It is a prejudiced formulated notion that male and female travellers have different access to places, and there are places and topography which are supposed not to be suitable for women to travel. Mary

Morris writes in *Virago Book of Women Travellers*, "women . . . move through the world differently than men,"[20] which is supported by Shirley Ardener, as she writes, "patriarchy created a 'social map' that constructed some spaces as 'feminine' and others as 'masculine,' using gender difference to inscribe 'spatial difference,' when women cross spatial, geographic boundaries their movement is seen as 'a threat to patriarchy and to the social order.'"[21] So when Dervla Murphy declares her intentions of travelling from Lismore to India on a bicycle, she clearly becomes guilty of breaking the social order of patriarchal mode of travelling. By travelling in threatening and dangerous situations all her life, Dervla has had transgressed protocols of women travelling alone. By planning and executing the entire travel from sending the four-spare wheel of Roz (as it is very difficult to find her wheels anywhere else) to different embassies, to taking all the decisions related to lodging and food, she has declared herself as an independent, strong figure who faced the extremes of hardship and severity with courage, without making any reference to 'feminine' concerns. Hence, Susan Bassnett is justified when she says of Dervla that her books are "firmly rooted in everyday experience and offer down-to-earth portraits of how she as an individual (not as a female traveller, emphasis mine), dealt both with physical hardship and social conscience." 2002: 240)

The way Murphy roams around the world courageously, proves the adage 'men travel in a completely different way than a woman'—a mythic interpretation of a prejudiced norm. I believe that every individual perceives things differently and travels the same place with a disparate perspective and looks at the same thing with a completely different viewpoint. Sometimes the motive and the reason with which one travels, to some extent, affect the way of looking at and perceiving the terrain travelled. Therefore, it's not 'who' travelled but 'why' travelled which effects the travel experiences and narratives and hence, it is not the gender but the motive and the reason for travelling which mostly affects the style and form of travel writing. As justly put by Alison in her seminal work, "Only a Woman," "Gender should not be seen in essentialist terms but rather as constructed and contested in many different ways over space and time."[22]

Therefore, travel writing is necessarily a product of a particular time and a particular culture. Sometimes even when women travellers produce the same kind of literature as their male counterpart, they have been judged by scholars and readers differently. For example, William Dalrymple's book on Delhi, *City of Djinns*, received a completely different and decent reception than Swapna Liddle's work on the same city, *Chandni Chowk: The Mughal City of Old Delhi*. Shirley Foster and Sara Mills justly argue that gender is only one variable amongst many, interacting constantly with other factors such as 'race, age, class, and financial position, education, political ideals and historical period.'[23]

But one noteworthy point is that, definitely in one case travel writer's gender plays an important role, which is, in the reception of travel account rather than the production. It has also been observed that even when men and women produce more or less identical forms of travel writing, their travelogues will often be received differently by reading public, on the account of the author's gender. As I have already mentioned in the case of Dalrymple and Liddle's work on Delhi, both works received different reception; gender, for sure, being one of the reasons.

Dervla Murphy's, generally all works and specifically, *Full Tilt: From Ireland to India with a Bicycle,* confirm Worley's observation that the texts written by women are different than men but not 'necessarily different because they were written by women, but that conventions have a determining role in the way a text is produced and judged.[24] Hence, *Full Tilt* underpinned the importance of gender as a factor which consistently makes a difference but not in a conventional codified way. Similarly, the notion that women are 'sessile' and don't travel is proved to be a norm, like the summation that women don't pen down their experiences of travelling but when it comes to reception and publication, women travel writers are pushed into the alley of anonymity. All these norms are strongly reflected in all works of Dervla Murphy. It is this reason why even after writing more than 20 travel books, little critical research is done on Dervla Murphy's works. If any male author would have written same number of travelogues as Dervla, he would have been a celebrated writer by now. So, I would like to conclude with the lines that Dervla Murphy is a travel legend who contests the very idea that "women can't be the hero of their narrative," and with her fierce independence, courage and self-determination proved herself to be the hero of *Full Tilt* and many more travel accounts she wrote later in her life.

NOTES

1. Susan Bassnett (2002), 'Travel Writing and Gender,' ed. Peter Hulme and Tim Youngs, *The Cambridge Companion to Travel Writing.* Cambridge: Cambridge University Press, 225.
2. Qtd. Patricia B. Salzman-Mitchell (2005). *A Web of Fantasies: Gaze, Image, and Gender in Ovid's Metamorphoses.* Columbus: Ohio State University Press, 2005.
3. Susan L. Roberson (2009), "American women and travel writing," Alfred Bendixen, Judith Hamera, ed. *Cambridge Companion to American Travel Writing,* Cambridge: Cambridge University Press, 214.
4. Paul Fussel (*Abroad: British Literary Travelling Between the Wars*, Oxford: Oxford University Press, 1980), Denis Porter (1990) and Peter Hulme (2002) have delineated women writers as a 'non-existent gender' in the genre of travel writing in their respective critical works *Abroad: British Literary Travelling Between the Wars, Haunted Journeys: Desires and Transgression in European Travel Writing*, and *The Cambridge Companion to Travel Writing.*
5. Carl Thompson (2009), "Question of Gender and Sexuality," *Travel Writing*. Cambridge: Cambridge University Press, 169.

6. Dervla Murphy (1967; 2010), "Introduction," *Full Tilt: Ireland to India with a Bicycle*, Eland Publishers, iv.
7. Clifford Graves, review of *Full Tilt* "The Perils of Dervla Murphy," 1969. https://cycling.ahands.org/bicycling/dervla.html
8. Leslie Blanch (1974), *The Wilder Shores of Love*, Panther, London. Qtd. Shirley Foster and Sara Mills (2002), ed. *An Anthology of Women's Travel Writing,* Manchester: Manchester Univ. Press, 35.
9. Jane Robinson (1990), *Wayward Women. A Guide to Women Travellers*. London: Oxford University Press, xiv.
10. Dervla Murphy's publishers and good friends, John and Diana Murray, after reading the script of *Wheels within the Wheels* had to cajole her for publishing her Autobiography, which according to Dervla, "I wrote it for Rachel, really, as I had a strange childhood that I wanted her to understand. I never expected it to be published—and I couldn't have written it if I'd thought it would be. But years later Jock Murray was rooting around and came across the old manuscript, and, in the way that publishers do, persuaded me we should put it out." https://www.telegraph.co.uk/travel/artsandculture/travelbooks/7865817/Dervla-Murphy-interview-Around-the-world-in-80-years.html
11. Foucault (1981b), 'The order of discourse,' qtd. L.K. Worley (1986), 'Through others' eyes; narratives of German women travelling in nineteenth century America,' *Yearbook of German-American Studies*, 21.
12. Dervla Murphy (2010), "Introduction," *Full Tilt: From Ireland to India With a Bicycle.* Eland Books, 14-15
13. Jeanne Denys and B. Norwick in their respective works, *Alexandra David-Neel au Tibet* and *Alexandra David-Neel's adventures in Tibet, fact or fiction* have criticized/ accused Alexandra David-Neel's travel work, *My Journey to Lhasa* (1927) as a work of exaggeration and falsehood. As studied by Sara Mills (1991), *Discourses of Difference: An analysis of women's travel writing and colonialism,* London & New York: Routledge, 123-50.
14. Garret Daly and Martina McGlynn are husband-wife duo, producer and director of 'Who is Dervla Murphy' (May 2016), a small documentary made on the life of Dervla Murphy. www.her.ie/

entertainment/who-is-dervla-murphy-brilliant-new-documentary-profiles-this-trailblazing-irish-woman-287841

15. Mariellen Ward (7 August 2017), "Going Full Tilt with Dervla Murphy," *Breathe Dream Go,* Online travel guide, https://breathedreamgo.com/go-books-full-tilt.html//
16. Hugh Thomson, "Dervla Murphy: Around the world in 80 years," Interview, 1 July 2010. *Telegraph.*, Online Magazine, https://www.telegraph.co.uk/travel/artsandculture/travelbooks/7865817/Dervla-Murphy-interview-Around-the-world-in-80-years.html
17. Rosamund Burton, "Travel writer Dervla Murphy tells her most harrowing story," Interview, *The Sydney Herald.*, Online Magazine, https://www.smh.com.au/entertainment/books/travel-writer-dervla-murphy-tells-her-most-harrowing-story-20150615-ghj7bk.html
18. Jane Robinson (1990), *Wayward Women. A Guide to Women Travellers.* London: Oxford University Press, xii.
19. Michel Kerr, "Dervla Murphy: 'Once travellers shared opinions and experiences—now they queue silently to use a computer,' Interview, *Telegraph,* Online Magazine, https://www.telegraph.co.uk/travel/books/Dervla-Murphy-Once-travellers-shared-opinions-and-experiences-now-they-queue-silently-to-use-a-computer
20. Mary Morris (1994; 2007), "Introduction," *The Illustrated Virago Book of Women Travellers*, London: Virago, ii.
21. Shirley Arder quoted in Alison Blunt and Gillian Rose (1994), ed. *Writing Women and Space: Colonial and Postcolonial Geographies,* New York and London: The Guilford Press, 1.
22. Alison Mary Blunt (1992), *Only a Woman. Women Travel Writers and Imperialism.* University of British Columbia, 14. Unpublished work.
23. Shirley Foster and Sara Mills. (2002), ed. *An Anthology of Women's Travel Writing*, Manchester: Manchester University Press, 1.
24. L.K. Worley, p. 44.

Travel Writing to Travel Literature: Journeys of Travel Narratives in Acquiring New Generic Identities

SUBARNA BHATTACHARYA
Symbiosis College of Arts and Commerce, Pune

Paul Fussell, an American cultural and literary historian and the writer of the award-winning book *The Great War and Modern Memory* (1975), in one of his other seminal works, *Abroad: British Literary Travelling Between the Wars* (1980), had observed that 'travel is now impossible and that tourism is all we have left.'[1] Fussell had made this comment as he was discussing British interwar travelling during the 1920s and 1930s, the decades he felt were crucial in bringing the change from 'exploration' to 'travel' to 'tourism.' In an age of globalization, there is really hardly any scope for 'travel' or 'exploration' in the old sense, what has taken its place is 'tourism' in the form of an organized industry. One may argue here that the homogenizing forces of globalization and the so-called cosmopolitan world we live in have killed the essence of 'travel' by eliminating the feeling of foreignness that a traveller would, in earlier times, experience during his or her travel. Therefore, in the context of all these cultural changes, writing about travel ought to be different as well. Travel stories about some heroic exploits or geographical explorations to an exotic locale have, of course, become things of the past. Travel writing, today, more than about the place or the locale is about the impact the journey has on the traveller/writer, written frequently in the form of a memoir or a personalized writing and often celebrated for its excessive interiority.

Although travel has been a common theme in literature, and that narratives of travel have been popular forms of writing and reading since many eras of the past, travel writing as a genre has not received serious academic attention until recently. Writing about travel, discourses on travellers's experiences abroad had remained a sub-genre until the resurgence of academic interest in travel writing around the last two decades of the twentieth century, when the genre began to receive a wide spectrum of critical attention from several humanist disciplines like Anthropology, Diaspora Studies, Cultural Studies, Postcolonial Studies and Gender Studies. Historically the time coincides with the years of the wars of liberation in many former European colonies, post the Second World War, which resulted in a huge flux of immigration and a consequent remapping of the world. As the twentieth century was rolling towards its mid-decades, not only volumes of travel increased, types of travel became greatly diversified. Now, the idea of 'travel,' more often than before, was replaced by the idea of 'displacement.' Notions like 'place' and 'destination' were redefined as 'space.' 'Home,' 'departure,' journey,' 'destination' lost their meaning and reference in this new world of diasporas and in the context of the new globalized world that ensued. The idea of travel in the current context began to be loaded with thick layers of meaning, which quite obviously necessitated the genre of travel writing to refashion itself and redirect its course. In the new trend of travel writing that thus emerged, 'places' have begun to be looked upon as 'imaginary spaces,' formed out of individual subjective realities. Travel texts have become complex representations of 'places' and the associated journeys, filtered through individual subjective consciousness. That travel writing is actually the representation of a place, or rather a space, whether as concrete or as imaginary construct is the new approach to study of travel writing today. Travel writing in the twentieth century acquired new generic identities, under the influence of the changing dynamics of a world slowly opening up to the processes of globalization and modern and post-modern cultural politics. In the course of this generic redirection, travel writing of the interwar years, that is the decade of the thirties, was especially remarkable. During this time, from being mere travelogues or traveller's accounts, the genre transformed itself to travel literature, more subjective and individualistic in style, and one in which several complex issues of critical interest emerge. As decades rolled by, twentieth century travel writing continued to be more and more complex, it being a genre to come easily under the influence of the phenomenon of 'globalization' and the ensuing cultural politics. From a subgenre mainly comprising of a corpus of utilitarian writing, it transformed into a genre, whether fully literary or not, but offering scope for serious academic reading and critical understanding.

Travel writing is a fluid genre, the problem of generic demarcation being one of its characteristic attributes. To put it in a term used by Barbara Korte,[2] it is an 'androgynous' literary form—a genre that has cross-overs with fiction, poetry, tales of pilgrimage, missionary accounts, scientific explorative reports, journalistic pieces. Hybridity in form, thus, has always been inherent in the genre. For instance, the medieval times and the early modern age are full of examples, when travel took the form of pilgrimage. Talking about travel and pilgrimage, one may quite obviously remember Chaucer here. Chaucer's *The Canterbury Tales* stands as a representative pilgrimage text of the medieval times to have a travel story as the main narrative frame. Another common motif in the genre of travel writing is that of a 'quest.' In many travel narratives, the idea of 'quest' appears as the central thread. The 'quest' can be a physical one, involving a journey of exploration to an unknown geographical region. The 'quest' can also be a metaphorical one, where it is actually an inward journey for some kind of a spiritual discovery. John Bunyan's *The Pilgrim's Progress* (1678), for instance, is a travel with a quest theme, where the journey is both a physical experience and a psychological or a spiritual exercise. However, neither *The Canterbury Tales* nor *The Pilgrim's Progress* can be called categorical travel works. Travel book's popularity as a genre started with travellers like Marco Polo travelling to Cathay (China) in the second half of the 13th century, Mandeville's *Travels,* Christopher Columbus's first voyage to America in 1492. Needless to say, these were the travel works of exploration and discovery, the narratives of 'quest' to some unknown geographical territory. This was the beginning of travel writing's own journey in search of a generic identity. It was also the point of beginning of Europe's construction of the cultural 'other.' The real problem for the travel writers of the time was the representational anxiety in constructing the 'New World' in the text for the readers back at home. It needed new expressions and startling language to depict this 'other.' Marco Polo in his *Travels*, portrays the mysterious east with sufficient amount of wonder and bizarre descriptions, which emphasizes the otherness of the natives by stressing the unfamiliarity of their appearance, their habits and their customs. I would quote a few lines from Marco Polo's *Travels*, where the traveller Marco Polo gives a detailed description of the inhabitants of Zanzibar: 'They are quite black and go about completely naked but for a loin-cloth. Their hair is so curly that they can only comb it when it is wet. They have wide mouths and turned-up noses. Their eyes and lips are so protuberant that they are a horrible sight. Anyone meeting them in another country would mistake them for devils.'[3]

A fundamental fictionality in representation is quite evident here and this underlines another important generic trait of travel writing, the mixing of objectivity and subjectivity in textual representation. Although generically all travel writing has to have a factual base and therefore claim to have accuracy of details and objectivity in presentation, writing we know can hardly be an objective medium of discourse. Moreover, in writing about travel, a space for the traveller-writer's perceptions, his individual and subjective responses to his travel experiences can hardly be denied or ruled out. Travel writings, thus, are always curious blends of objective presentations of facts and details and their subjective representations.

Moving on to the early modern age travel writing, which was primarily utilitarian in purpose, works like Richard Hakluyt's collection, *Principal Navigations, Voyages, Traffics, and Discoveries of the English Nation* (1589) were rather factual than fictional, as travel at this time was mostly of explorative or mercantile type. It now assumed the form of 'reportage.' A report meant a chronological narrative of the expedition undertaken, with geographical and ethnographical findings and observations. Reports were sometimes substantiated with detailed maps and more frequently with sets of instructions for future travellers.[4] Such form of 'reportage' found mostly in the travel works of the Renaissance and early modern age continued to be widely used even in the 19th century, when it became an all the more popular form for the colonialist imperialist travel projects undertaken by Europe.

So travel writing, till the 1900, was a genre with frequent overlaps with scientific reports or documentative kind of writing. Post 1900s, however, several factors started dominating, influencing and shaping travel writing. So coming now to the context of the twentieth century, the formative years which, I argue, shaped travel writing's course to the present day were the decades of the 1920s and 1930s, the time when many eminent literary figures of the time undertook to travel and wrote about their experiences. Among them were novelists like D.H. Lawrence, Wyndham Lewis, Graham Greene, George Orwell, Evelyn Waugh, Christopher Isherwood, Rebecca West and even poets like W.H. Auden, and Louis MacNeice, whom Paul Fussell in his book *Abroad: British Literary Travel Writing between the Wars*, refers to as the 'British Literary Diaspora of the 1920s and 1930s.'[5] Not only did they write about their journeys in their travel works, they also explored the significance of 'travel' or 'journeys' in their fiction and poetry. Naturally, in the hands of these novelists and poets, travel writing was infused with literary qualities. Not being originally a literary genre itself, travel writing now opens up more and more to extensive use of metaphors, fragmented and disjunctive narratives and other stylistic devices of canonical modernist literature. This was the beginning of a new journey for the genre of travel writing—the process of its acquiring new generic identities and refashioning itself as travel literature. It was a time when, due to several reasons, socio-political or otherwise, all of a sudden, there was a common perception among the sensitive thinkers and intellectuals of the tome about 'reality' being disjointed, dissociated and fractured. This undoubtedly called forth the urgent necessity to device newer experimental techniques for representations of realities in modernist texts. Similar literary experiments were conducted in the genre of travel writing as well, which resulted in such travel books as Christopher Isherwood and W.H. Auden's *Journey to a War (*1939), Louis MacNeice's *I Crossed the Minch* (1939), MacNeice and Auden's *Letters from Iceland* (1937), Robert Byron's *The Road to Oxiana* (1937), Rebecca West's *Black Lamb and Grey Falcon: A Journey through Yugoslavia* (1944) and many more.

In the context of the twentieth century, there hardly was a time before this when non-literary phenomena were so conspicuous in influencing and producing the literature of the time. First, the time saw the beginning and the gradual ripening of what we may call the 'Petrol Age,' with great advancements in road and railway network, facilitating a boom time in travel. Some were mass-travel and some highly individualistic travel. Mass-travel was often motivated by political reasons (one must not forget here the political scenario of extremist Leftist and Rightist politics dominating the Continent at that time) and sometimes due to economic reasons, like unemployment. The political geography of Europe in the post First World War years was changing, resulting in migration and displacement, the outcome of which was a great upsurge of metropolitan diasporic population in all the important cities of

Western Europe. In the late thirties, a major percentage of displaced population comprised of immigrants who fled from Hitler's Germany. Besides all these, there was leisure travel, both over long and short distances. The ease of locomotion brought the advent of the tourism industry which popularized commercially organized group travels at minimized costs. However, travel at this time was more diversified than only this. People undertook to travel individually as well, sometimes for professional reasons, as it was in the case of the journalists, or simply for the sake of writing about travel. Paul Fussell, quite interestingly, observes three different forms of travel in the thirties. He distinguishes between 'explorer,' 'traveller' and 'tourist' by pointing out that the explorer 'seeks the undiscovered,' whereas the tourist seeks that which has been discovered by business. The traveller occupies a place in between these two, 'retaining all he can of the excitement of the unpredictable attaching to exploration, and fusing that with the pleasure of "knowing where one is" belonging to tourism.'[6]

So, not only in the business of tourism, twentieth century saw an increase in number of travellers pursuing individualistic travels, sometimes as journalistic ventures, sometimes on literary projects, sometimes even motivated by political preferences. For instance, Greene travelled to Liberia and then to Mexico. Orwell travelled to Spain during the Spanish Civil War. Evelyn Waugh travelled along the Mediterranean coast, and also, to Mexico and Africa. W.H. Auden with Christopher Isherwood went to China and with Louis MacNeice travelled to Iceland. It should be noted that most of these writers travelled under the impulse of their own ideological convictions and most of the time their choice of destinations for travel were based on their political preferences. It is not surprising, therefore, that we have Orwell travelling to Spain and Auden and MacNeice travelling to China. These politically motivated ideologically driven travels form a significant corpus of early twentieth century travel writing, something which Bernard Schweizer discusses at length in his book *Radicalson the Road*.[7]

Another significant influence on travel writing of the twentieth century was the emerging field of media technology. During the 1920s and 1930s, the first gift from the new media technology was the radio, and then the talking picture. These developments in mass media attracted even literary people towards it. For example, one style of cinema that particular attracted W.H. Auden was the documentary. The 1930s also initiated the age of photojournalism, what Samuel Hynes in his seminal study *The Auden Generation*[8] calls 'feature-journalism.' Print journalism became an attractive choice for employment and even notable figures of the time, like Evelyn Waugh and Graham Greene were closely associated with it. Alongside print journalism, there was also photojournalism, that is, use of photography for news coverage. As documentary films, photography and photo-journalism began to be used as new tools for reproduction of realities in art and they succeeded in attracting significant literary figures of the time like W.H. Auden to the newly emergent media technology, one can possibly say that the conservatism of 'high' art slowly was beginning to merge in with the popular culture and popular forms of communication. As travel became diversified now with the reasons for travel becoming more and more varied, travel writing also broadened its spectrum to share grounds with other emerging forms like journalistic writing, photojournalism, war-writing and documentaries. The experimental mood of the age, which was already so very evident in the mainstream literatures of the modernist writers of the time, was reiterated in these emerging forms—of them, travel writing being a significant one.

A reference to one of the most unconventional and path-breaking yet less known travel works of the time, the *Letters to Iceland* (1937) may help to establish the point in question. The book *Letters to Iceland* was W.H. Auden's collaborative travel piece with Louis MacNeice. About *Letters* Auden says, 'It is a collage that you are going to read,' and uses a form which is fragmented and discontinuous, the narrative comprising of a bunch of letters, a few poems, and 'photographs,/Some out of focus, some with wrong exposures,/Press cuttings, gossip, maps, statistics, graphs.'[9] The disjunction in form that he achieves by the mixing of genres helps in dislocating perspectives, the result being a very innovative form of a travel book, something which Stan Smith describes as a book that 'plays deliberate games with the travelogue format.'[10] Neither do we find the traditional story telling of a travel book, nor the travel writer's promise of bringing to his readers some bizarre experiences he had during travel. Pointing out the fact that just before their Icelandic trip Auden had been involved in a six month's job with a documentary film, critic Marsha Bryant says (about *Letters to Iceland*), 'Auden's first-hand experience with film made him aware of the politics of visual representation, so that he experimented with camera framing and with collage form in order to blur the line between observer and observed in *Letters from Iceland.*'[11]

What Auden and MacNeice in the book mean to question is the fundamental claim made by conventional travel writing, that of authenticity of factual representation. Auden builds multi-perspectivism in the narrative, sometimes through jarring camera effects, sometimes by using strange focal points in the photographs and sometimes by diffusing the focus of the camera altogether. These techniques help in destabilizing perspectives even more than they destroy any authoritative gaze of the traveller using camera. The experimentations in formal techniques and the seriocomic mode of presentation attribute a kind of self-consciousness to the travel work about its mode of representation. By these, Auden raises questions about the so-called objectivism of all these genres like travel writing, documentary writing, photography, and photojournalism and thereby exposes their limits as well. Auden and MacNeice's *Letters from Iceland* was not the only example of such experimentation with forms. Many modernist travel writings experimented with forms, played with the shifting points of view technique, examined the relationship between observers and observed and questioned the authority conventionally assumed by the traveller persona in a travel book.

The formal experimentations, which the modernist travel writing of the 1920s and 1930s started, continued to determine the course of the development of the genre for the rest of the twentieth century. Even for the later travel writers like Paul Theroux, Patrick Leigh Fermor and Eric Newby the genre has been one in which the writer may take the liberty to play with the ideas of self, of authority and of artistic representation. Again and again there is a kind of proclamation from the travel writers that the knowledge being shared through the travel work could be partial, incomplete and subject to the traveller's individual perception. In the author's note to *The Lawless Roads*, we find Greene saying, 'This is the personal impression of a small part of Mexico at a particular time, the spring of 1938.'[12] Auden and MacNeice do the same in *Letters from Iceland*. In the Preface to the book, Auden says, 'A travel book owes so little to the writers and so much to the people they meet, that a full and fair acknowledgment on the part of the former is impossible. We must beg those hundreds of anonymous Ice-landers, farmers, fishermen, busmen, children, etc., who are the real authors of this book to accept collectively our gratitude.'[13]

There is a deliberate undercutting of the traveller's authority here as a person speaking about or representing a place. This characteristic unsettling of authority in travel writing, which started at this time, continued in later modern or post-modern Anglo-American travel writing as well. Paul Theroux's *The Great Railway Bazaar: By Train Through Asia* (1975) is often considered a classic in the genre. A journalistic, yet a very introspective style in travel writing, adopted by travel writers like Wilfred Thesiger, Norman Lewis, Peter Matthiesen and Bruce Chatwin brought in newer experiments in form. Works like Norman Lewis's *A Dragon Apparent: Travels in Indo-China* (1951), Matthiessen's *The Snow Leopard* (1978) and Bruce Chatwin's *In Patagonia* (1977) and *The Songlines* (1987) can be said to have completely reworked the genre. They reverse the focus from the 'place' visited to the travelling persona of the author, bring in a space for subjectivity in the whole experience of travelling and writing and complicate the relationship of the observer and the observed.

Another noticeable fact in the case of European travel writing is that, since the time of the Renaissance, travel writing had engaged in the very traditional role of the western construction of the cultural 'other.' Till the end of the nineteenth century and even in the early twentieth century, European travel writing had consistently been imperialistic, the reason being its close association with colonialist explorative projects, especially in the continent of Africa or in the Far East. Travel writing therefore has always been looked upon as a discourse involving in the process of knowledge production about the 'other,' producing colonial stereotypes, travelogues being an essentially imperialist mode of representation. Early twentieth century travel writing, and especially that of the 1930s, was unique in the sense that more than involving in the construction of the cultural 'other,' the travel works of this time engaged in the construction of the 'self.' It is the foregrounding of the self in these writing that makes these travel works more introspective, inward-looking and more reflective. Written during the years of imperial dissolution and simultaneous political instability at home, they present sympathetic and complex subject positions, which become more complicated in relation to the external world. By the end of the first two decades of the twentieth century, Europe had reached the climax of territorial colonialism and it was the very process of colonialism which resulted in things like transculturation and miscegenation, migration and displacement. Travel writing took a generic redirection. It was increasingly becoming aware of these realities being produced all over beyond Europe through the processes of colonialism and the multiple effects of transculturation, migration and displacement. The travel books of the interwar years were thus the first to register this consciousness of cultural heterogeneity and therefore, they present starkly different dynamics.

The travel texts of this time of imperial dissolution, in a way, also anticipated future re-workings in the genre, bringing in new generic diversifications like post-colonial travel writings, such as V.S. Naipaul's *The Middle Passage* (1962), which would be narratives of reverse travel by descendants of colonized subjects, or even women's travel writing, with some exceptional works by women travel writers like Isabella Bird, Rebecca West and Freya Stark. Travel writing is and has been a continually evolving genre. As on one hand, it has all the attributes to belong to the category of popular reading and popular culture, on the other hand, it is a genre of writing frequently considered for serious academic studies like studies in culture and cultural politics. In the context of twentieth century globalization and global geopolitics, travel and writing about travel, thus, continue to thrill us in terms of both popular readership and critical and theoretical scholarship.

NOTES

1. Paul Fussell, *Abroad. British Literary Traveling Between the Wars* (New York: Oxford University Press, 1980) p.41.
2. Barbara Korte, *English Travel Writing: From Pilgrimages to Post-Colonial Explorations*, trans. Catherine Matthias (Great Britain: Macmillan Press Ltd., U.S.A.: St. Martin's Press, INC., 2000) p. 9.
3. Marco Polo, *The Travels of Marco Polo*, trans. Teresa Waugh (London: Sidgwick and Jackson, 1984) p. 175, as quoted in Casey Blanton, *Travel Writing. The Self and the World* (New York: Twayne Publishers, 1997) p. 7.
4. One reason why maps were rare was that the competing nations required keeping their trade routes secret. However, with the increasing popularity of travel books, hand sketches of maps, showing important cities and ports, even sometimes native costumes and regional flora and fauna began to appear.
5. Paul Fussell.

6. *Ibid.*, p. 39.
7. Bernard Schweizer, *Radicals on the Road: The Politics of English Travel Writing in the 1930s (*Richmond: University Press of Virginia, 2001)
8. Samuel Hynes, *The Auden Generation: Literature and Politics in England in the 1930s (*Great Britain: Bodley Head, 1976)
9. W.H. Auden and Louis MacNeice, *Letters from Iceland.* 1937 (London: Faber & Faber, 1973) p. 21.
10. Stan Smith, 'Burbank with a Baedeker,' p. 6, qtd. Tim Young, *The Cambridge Introduction to Travel Writing* (Cambridge: Cambridge University Press, 2013) p.72.
11. Marsha Bryant, *Auden and Documentary in the 1930s* (Charlottesville: University Press of Virginia, 1997) p.77.
12. Graham Greene, *The Lawless Roads* (Harmondsworth: Penguin Books 1947. London: William Heinemann Ltd., 1955) Author's Note.
13. Auden and MacNeice, *Letters from Iceland.* 1937, Preface.

John Donne as a Poet of '*Dhvani*'

RICHA BISWAL
University of Allahabad, Allahabad

Dhvani Sampradāya is the most celebrated school of Indian poetics propounded by Anandavardhana in the 9th century and further nourished by Abhinavagupta, Ruyyaka, Mammata, Pt. Rāja Jagganatha and Vishvanātha. In this school, the skill of the poet relies on interpreting the same stanza in five or six different ways which indicates the richness of a language and the skill of the poet in conveying the meaning. *Dhvani* has got several layers of meaning. Just as the stick put in water goes on creating ripples or circles one after another, in the same way circles or layers of meaning can be seen in a text where the theory of *dhvani* is applied.

The word *dhvani* in Sanskrit literally means "echo." According to this school, the artistic enjöyment from literary works is achieved not by the images that are created by the direct meaning of the words but by the associations and ideas evoked by those images. The direct images are called *vāchya* (the stated) and the indirect images are called *pratiyamāna* (the implied) and are perceived only by those who know the meaning of poetry. Anandavardhana elaborated his theory of *dhvani* in his book *Dhvanyāloka,* on which later Abhinavagupta wrote a commentary entitled *Dhvanyāloka-Lochana.* Anandavardhana has made a comparative study of different schools of criticism in *Dhvanyāloka* and has established *dhvani* theory as the most valid theory. The whole *dhvani* theory of Anandavardhana is based on the concept of *vyanjaktā* (suggestiveness). We know that the

Indian tradition of poetics accepts three types of meaning emanating from *śabdaśakti* (word-power): 1. *Vācyartha* or *abhidheyārtha* (denotative or primary meaning) 2. *Laksyārtha* or *laksaṇā* (implicative, secondary or derivative meaning) and 3. *Vyaṅgyārtha* or *dhvanyārtha* (suggestive or tertiary meaning). The last one is declared as *dhvani. Vāchayartha* is the bold or literal meaning, *lakshyārtha* is the metaphorical meaning and *dhvanyārtha* is the suggestive meaning. Suggestiveness can be located in syllables, words, sentences, diction and even in the whole poetry as well as in its arrangement. According to Mahimabhatta, *abhidhā* (primary meaning) is the chief power of words in which *vyanjanā* (tertiary or suggested meaning) is always latent. As we delve deep into *abhidhā*, we get the meaning of *vyanjanā.* Just as an arrow penetrates the skin and reaches the heart, the literal meaning goes deep beneath its surface meaning to convey *vyaṅgyārtha.* As far as *laksaṇā* is concerned, it is the suppression of the *mukhyārthabhidhā* (literal meaning). *Laksaṇā* is based on *sāmpiyasambandha* (mutual closeness between words), *sādrśya* (similarity), *samvāya* (association), *vaiparitya* (contrast), *kṛyā yoga (*attribution). Thus *laksaṇā* works very powerfully in language. Like *laksaṇā, vyanjanā* is also opulent and plays a decisive role in language. It mysteriously exposes a new sense other than the conventional one.

Anandavardhana starts his work with the motto 'suggestion is the soul of poetry.' This concept is encapsulated in his maxim '*kāvyasyātmadhvani.*' Then to remove all confusion about the new concept and to give pleasure to the sensitive readers he defines *dhvani* as that type of poetry where the expression and the literal meaning keep themselves subordinate and reveal the suggested meaning which is most important. He has also stated that the soul of poetry is the *pratiyamānartha* (suggested meaning). Concealment is the essence of *vyanjanā*. In poetry, only the implicit, indirect and suggested meaning is capable of producing beauty. Abhinavagupta says that the term *dhvani* can be interpreted in five different ways: the suggestive expression (conventional symbol—the articulate sound), the suggestive literal meaning (conventional meaning), the suggested meaning (the power of word to convey the suggestive meaning), a type of suggested poetry (the suggestive meaning) and the function of suggestion (poetic work containing the suggestive element). Of these Anandavardhana seems to have used the term in the sense of the suggested meaning and the type of suggestive poetry. The importance of this theory was taken up later by Bhattanayaka, Abhinavagupta and others. Bhattanayaka attacks the *dhvani* theory by saying that it is the *vyāpāra* or function. Mahimabhatta's attempt to prove that all types of *dhvani* comes under *anumāna* (inference) shows that he took *dhvani* as a *vyāpāra*. So the main problem now is whether *dhvani* is a *vyapara* (function) or the suggested meaning. Ruyyaka has stated that Anandavardhana took the suggested meaning as the soul of poetry, whereas Kuntaka and Bhattanayaka took the *vyāpāra* (function) as most important. Generally only three senses are ascribed to *dhvani*: the suggestive operation, the suggested meaning and suggestive poetry. Mahimabhatta repudiated *dhvanisiddhānta*. He argued that the entire *dhvanivāda* was merely an inference based on imagination, but Abhinavagupta gave mature interpretative shape to *dhvanisiddhānta*. Mammata gave a proper positive explanation refuting the counter arguments of earlier critics. Hemachandra, Vishvanātha and lastly Panditarāja Jagannātha were strong supporters of *dhvanisiddhānta*.

A close analysis of the minute details of the *dhvani* theory reveals, as Vishvanātha has shown, 5355 subdivisions of suggestive poetry. Anandavardhana follows the binary division. According to him, *dhvani* (suggestion) can be based on either words or meanings and therefore, suggestion is broadly classified into two types: *sabdanishtha* (as that occurring in words) and *arthanishtha* (as that occurring in word-meanings). *Sabdanishtha* is classified further into two kinds: *avivaksitavācya* (unintended denotation i.e. suggestion wherein primary expressed meaning or sense is not the one intended) and *vivaksitanyaparāvāchya* (extended denotation i.e. suggestion wherein primary expressed meaning is intended but is subordinate to the actually implied meaning i.e. along with the literal meaning something more is intended). The first is based on *laksaṇā* or indication, and the second on *abidhā* or denotation. The *laksaṇā* born *dhvani* is again of two kinds: *arthāntarasamkramit-avācya* (suggestion where the primary, expressed, literal sense and meaning pass or shift into another sense or implied actual meaning) and *atyantatiraskrtavācya* (suggestion where the expressed sense or the literal and primary meaning disappears entirely or it is set aside, rejected and ignored completely). Both of these types are divided as *pādaprakāsya* (manifest in a word) or *vākyaprakāsya* (manifest in a sentence). The *vivaksitan-yapāravācya* type of suggestion, which is based on the denotative or expressive power of words, conveys an extraordinary sense of beauty by making the primary expressed meaning totally subordinate to the other actually implied meaning. This *abhidhā* born *dhvani* is also subdivided into two categories: *asam-laksyakramavyangya* (that in which the suggested meaning is of an imperceptible process) and *samlaksyakramavyangya* (that in which the suggested meaning is of a perceptible process). The main difference between *asamlaksyakrama* and *samlaksyakrama* is that the former includes the suggestion of *rasa* or relish or some *bhava* or emotional state suggested in a particular way. It suggests a particular sentiment based on the *bhāvas* and *rasa* in poetry. The latter includes the suggestion of *vastu* (matter/fact) and *alamkāra* (figure). The credit goes to Anandavardhana for reviving the concept of *rasa* first enunciated by Bharata in *Nātyashāstra* and extending it to literature in general and poetry in particular. The process by which the *rasa* or the effective response of the perceptive reader is manifested is, according to Anandavardhana, basically a process of suggestion. *Bhāva-dhvani* (pertaining to the transient emotion) is also a part of *asamlaksyakrama*. The subjective constituents of the aesthetic configuration, the mental states, are divided into two classes, the basic mental states or durable emotions and the transient emotions. Accordingly, we have *bhava-dhvani* when the idea suggested is a transient emotion.

Rasa-dhvani (pertaining to the aesthetic configuration) is considered to be the ultimate in poetic communication and is that revealing power which floods the mind with a host of ideas, not always clearly definable but necessary for the completion of an aesthetic image. It is also necessary for revealing the basic mental state at a high pitch and for bringing about complete self-forgetfulness in the hearer or reader. It consists in suggesting *bhāva* (feelings or sentiments). In *rasa-dhvani* emotion is conveyed through *vyanjaka. Rasa* is the subject of *vyanjakas* as differentiated from *abhidhā* and *lakṣaṇā*. Its cognition is almost simultaneous with the expressed. The *vyanjanās* (suggestions) are the objective correlatives of the response of the reader. The variety of *dhvani* possible in all poetry is *rasa-dhvani.* According to Abhinavagupta this alone is genuine *dhvani.* He holds that *rasa-dhvani* alone constitutes the soul of poetry. Both *vāstu-dhvani* and *alankāra-dhvani* finally merge into *rasa-dhvani.* Abhinavagupta has tried to list all varieties of *dhvani* in a mathematical way. He gives thirty-five varieties of *dhvani.* According to both Anandavardhana and Abhinavagupta, the language of great poetry is not explicit, but implicit and that the soul of great poetry is implicit rasa or rasa that is suggestive. *Asamlaksyakarmavyangya,* wherein the order of obtaining the suggestion from primary meaning is not perceived or is vague. In this type of *dhvani, rasas, bhāvas, rasābhāsa, bhāvabhāsa* etc. are suggested. *Samlaksyakramavyangya* has three varieties: *sabdasaktimulaka* (suggested by a particular word and based on the power/capacity of expression and words). It can be defined as the suggestion which brings out the restricted meaning. *Sabdasaktimulaka* involves double entendre; there is difference of opinion among commentators regarding this variety, since Anandavardhana's text is a bit ambiguous. According to Anandavardhana this type applies only where figures of speech are involved; but Abhinavagupta and Mammata accepted *vāstu* (idea) as coming under this type. In the case of double entendre where two kinds of meaning are conveyed: contextual and non-contextual; the non-contextual ideas are prevented from being grasped, because of restriction by contextual factors and only the contextual meaning is expressed directly. The understanding of the non-contextual meaning is attributed to suggestion in such cases according to Abhinavagupta and Mammata. Anandvardhana considers both the meanings as received through the primary denotative power itself; and the figure of speech like simile or contrast is conveyed by the suggestive power of the expression. *Arthasaktimula* (suggested by fact or figure and based on the content or literal sense i.e. word-meaning). It can be defined as the suggestion which brings out the transient feelings with the help of the expressed meanings. It is based on the content, expressed meanings and the suggested meaning. It can be a fact, a figure of speech or emotions and transient feelings. Thus there can be three varieties of this type: *vāstu-dhvani, alankāra-dhvani* and *rasā-dhvani*. The *arthasaktimula* type of *dhvani* can be divided into two varieties: 1. *Svatah-sambhāvi* or feasible in itself and 2. *Praudhoktimātranispannasarira* based on imagination and poetic fancy; the latter can be the fancy of the poet or that of a character created by the poet (*kavinibadhavaktrpraudhoktimatranispannasarira* and *kavipraudhoktimātrani-spannasarira*). There is also a combination of the two i.e. *ubhayasaktimula* or *sabdārthamula* based on both the expression and the literal meaning i.e. on both word and fact. It is added by the later writers. This *arthasaktimula* thus is of two kinds: *vāstu-dhvani* (suggestion of fact, meaning the suggestion which arises out of the primary meaning or an ordinary subject matter) is the revealing power, which operates to arouse the revealed meaning. This power (1) may arouse a negative meaning when the statement, in strict conventional sense, is positive or vice versa. (2) It may give rise to a meaning, which is neither positive nor negative, when the statement is clearly positive or negative.

(3) Or when the statement is meant not for the one, to whom it is addressed, but for the other, to whom the situation, in which the person addressed is involved, has to be explained in order that the latter may spare the former; it may give rise to a meaning quite different from that which the statement has for the addressed.

Thus, depending on the situation, the skill of the speaker and the capacity of understanding and visualization of the hearer, this power of revealing gives rise to innumerable meanings. The constituents of the aesthetic configuration can be divided into two classes, the objective and the subjective. By the objective is meant those, which represent something that exists outside the mind. And by subjective is meant mental states. The objective is further divided into two kinds: if it stimulates an emotion or if it indicates any mental states by gestures or facial expressions. The former is called *vibhāva* and the latter *anubhāva*. A meaning that refers to what is objective of either kind is included in the *vāstu-dhvani* and *alānkar-dhvani*. *Alankāra-dhvani* is that linguistic power or capacity suggesting an idea, which is a poetic embellishment.

The distinctions go on almost endlessly, but Anandavardhana takes adequate care to illustrate different kinds of *dhvani*. When *dhvani* is applied, the language becomes emotive, ambiguous, non-logical and open to multiple interpretations. It is the supreme glory of language that yields an infinite variety of meaning, so that poetry can transcend the descriptive and become suggestive and evocative. This is because the suggested sense given out by word always depends on the power of imagination of the poet and the suggested power of the word.

The theory of *dhvani* owes its inspiration to the grammarians in general and Bhartrhari in particular, and thus has a relation with the theory of *sphota*. The eternal sound unit, according to Bhartrhari is *sphota* and that alone can convey ideas. It is thus on the one hand manifested by letters and on the other an entity from which the sense comes out. There are various kinds of *sphota: varnasphota, vākyasphota* etc. A word expresses a sense not separately by its letters, which make up the word but in its entirety. Thus only when the word is complete the meaning emerges. The grammarians believe that a sentence is indivisible, and this means that a word will acquire a full sense only when the sentence is complete: by its original denotation and connotation and its position that the word occupies in the syntactic structure of a sentence. From these ideas developed the theory of *dhvani*. The term *dhvani* indicates the sound emanating from each letter during articulation and then mingling with the next sound and so on, finally creating a complete word with its denotation and connotation. The *alamkārikas* also use the term *dhvani* to signify suggestive word and meaning. The grammarians speak of different kinds of *dhvani* depending on whether it is short or long, soft or harsh, quick or slow. So the word *dhvani* can be derived in different ways:

(a) *dhvanatiitidhvani*—that which suggests (both 'word' and 'meaning' can be *dhvani* in this sense).

(b) *dhvanvatāitidhvani*—that which is suggested (only 'sense' comes under *dhvani* here).

(c) *dhvanānamdhvani*—the process of suggestion.

(d) *dhvanisamudāyahdhvanihkāvyam*—the entire literature formed out of the elements of *dhvani.*

However, Anandavardhana does not mean to suggest that words and primary meanings are unimportant. The expressed meaning is important; yet the suggested meaning remains the all-important thing. *Dhvani* flashes into the mind of the aesthetically sensitive listener. *Dhvani* theory describes the significant range of a word or an utterance, and Anandvardhana understood it as a step beyond both literal and metaphorical meanings. *Dhvani* is the inferred or alluded meaning hidden behind the generally accepted meaning of the word or word combination used. This mode of expression existed as an accepted fact already in literature. Dandin, Bhamaha, Udbhatta were fully aware of this suggestive mode of expression, nonetheless they had not explicitly dilated upon it in their treatises. They had given indication of this suggestive meaning while explaining *alankāras* like *paryokti, vyājastuti* etc.

II

Dhvani can be well compared to wit as *dhvani* does the same thing as wit. As wit is the clever and apt expression of words and ideas creating connections between dissimilar ideas to create pleasure, so is *dhvani*. To get a better understanding of the poetic wit used by Donne, the conventional description of *dhvani* may be extended and refreshed. Donne's poems have plenty of wit. Donne's use of wit proves that manner matters more than the subject. Donne's wit is full of strange ideas, imagination, thought and agility. It is deliberate and peculiar. Wit comes to Donne naturally because of his expansive knowledge and deep scholarship. His wit is scholastic and significant. His wit expresses all moods from optimistic to pessimistic. It is produced when he compares things that are apparently unlike. Wit can be seen in Donne's poetry when he uses special figures such as paradoxes, hyperboles, word-play, pun etc. to produce special effects, when he compresses thought and imagery, when he produces speech rhythms in complex versification, when he turns a thought into experience and when he creates intellectual pleasure.

Donne has been praised widely as a poet of wit by several critics like Theobold, Dryden, Pope, Coleridge, De Quincey, Saintsbury, Grierson, and Eliot. According to the modern critics Donne's poetry is the poetry of wit; his poetry uses the intellect to build up complex unities of thought out of non-poetic elements.

According to Thomas Carew, Donne was the king of the universal monarchy of wit. Dryden says that Donne had the greatest wit but he was not the greatest poet of our nation. Pope says that Donne had as much wit as any writer can possibly have but he had no imagination. De Quincey considers Donne's wit as the instrument of a mind which is subtle, ingenious and poetical. De Quincey contends that the rhetoric is the measure of Donne's successful style and wit. Costaine Hugghens, a Dutch poet and scholar, wrote to his friend and fellow poet Hoof that Donne is most famous because of his wit only. According to him many rich fruits from the green branches of his wit are enjoyed by the lovers of arts. Johnson suggests that wit of Donne can be seen in a combination of dissimilar images. He draws resemblances in things that are unlike. Theobold is of the view that Donne's wit is nothing but a continued heap of riddle. B.L. Joseph has defined Donne's wit as the mental ability to perceive fundamental relationships among different things, to represent his special insight in compressed but startling analogies, and to develop complex things in a few words, maintaining a colloquial air in complex versification.

Coleridge regards that Donne's wit has wonder and peculiarity of thought. According to him, to read Dryden, Pope etc. one only needs to count syllables but to read Donne one must measure time, and discover the time of each word by the sense of passion. Donne's wit surprises us with its intellectual agility. There is a fusion of emotion and thought in his wit and it comes to him through his learning. According to Leishman, it was Donne's wit that the Caroline poets tried to emulate and not his music, passion and dramatic force. Leishman holds that, the leading quality of Donne's poetry is wit and not his learning. He says Donne's wit lies in his imprudent and shocking language. For Leishman, Donne's dialectic is simplified and his wit is coarsened (71). Donne's dialectic is more ingenious, more various and more far-fetched due to which many of his poems have a very strong element of sheer wit, sheer invention and paradox (82). Though Ben Jonson's own practice was very different from Donne but he admired Donne's wit.

T.S. Eliot is of the view that Donne's wit is a blend of thought and feeling. He says it is a union of opposites, but it is a union of opposite faculties and not merely opposite concepts. A.J. Smith suggests that Donne's wit exhibits a cool sanity and a wary openness of thought which goes beyond the refusal of facile commitments of sardonic amusements. Grierson writes that Donne's wit followed no fashion, it was the natural working of a mind that is abnormally quick to apprehend likeness in things that are divergent. He considers that from his multifarious learning and analogies, wit came into Donne's head thick and fast. Grierson says because of Donne's wit, range, character, erudition and ingenuity, he is followed by the critics of all generations. Donne's satire, love songs and elegies are witty and lucid. The quality of Donne's poetry which made it the fashion of an age is his metaphysical wit. Donne's wit can be seen in the fantastic elaboration of one or two common moods, i.e. of compliment, passion, devotion and penitence (15).

Cleanth Brooks is of the view that Donne's wit is characterized by a complexity of moods and attitudes reflecting his perception of the complexity and intricacy of life. Donne's wit expresses all the moods and tones, ranging from the gay and playful to the dark and cynical. Brooks considers Donne to be a witty poet because of his use of metaphor and because of the images which he draws from the farthest possible distances. George Saintsbury is correct in saying that Donne's mind has every power that can be attained i.e. wit, insight, imagination etc. and whatever be the age whether medieval, renaissance or modern it is interesting (xi-xxxiii).

Emile Legouis aptly remarks that in Donne, wit is everywhere. It is his very genius, which fashions his feelings and his thought. Donne subordinates to wit in respect to passion, sentiment and sensuality. Albert C. Labriola points out that Ben Jonson in his epigram 'To John Donne' focused on the wit in the songs, sonnets and elegies of Donne. Jonson conveys through the epigram that Donne's wit shows his great mental capacity, intellectual ability, genius, talent, cleverness, mental quickness and sharpness (708). According to Haskin, Coleridge praised Donne as a logician, whose unique power of reasoning was informed by vigorous energy, thereby generating witty conceits that elicited both admiration and awe (52-58).

In her essay "The Metaphysical Poets," Helen Gardner writes argument, persuasions and use of conceits are the instruments of Donne's poems of wit. The conceit explicates whatever the poem has to say (57). The sense of the passionate moment and the aptness and incongruity of comparisons gives Donne's wit, its brilliance. Without this, as in some of his complimentary pieces, he labors to be witty (58). Donne's poems of wit have certain pungency in their thought, and their turns of phrase, whether profound or flippant, deserve the praise of being 'fine and wittie' (62). According to Warren the qualities in Donne's poems of wit are the desire to draw correspondences between heterogeneous things and thereby reveal the unity of what appears fragmentary (69).

Joseph Anthony Mazzeo writes that our own time is less witty than the time of Donne, and universal analogy has passed out of existence as a common habit of thought; the difficulty we have in penetrating this view of the world from within and somehow understanding it as 'natural' and not 'perverse' is, perhaps, the most important reason of all the confusion about the nature of the poetry of wit (72).

Murray Roston points out that Donne's impudent wit was carried over even into his ecclesiastical period (8). His wit can perhaps be best appreciated by comparing it with the wit of eighteenth century as Neo-classical poets also employ at times the technique of an initially incongruous juxtaposition, but they elicited totally different response from the reader. They carefully evoke a surface and momentary delight in an amused pretence which is then immediately resolved, in contrast to Donne's revelation of authentic and lasting paradox. Baltaser Gracian in his essay "Conceit and the Art of Wit" says that there exists a form of wit which consists more in the words, in such a way that if one departs from them, the meaning does not disappear, and they can be translated into another language (76). Donne's blend of piquant wit and religious commitment is uniquely his own (85). Donne's poetic wit, with his grotesque juxtapositions and deceptive reasoning, offered a perfect medium for expressing that mistrust of the objective (107). One of the main delights in Donne's specific form of wit is the agile elusiveness with which he tacks and veers in order to trap us intellectually just as we are congratulating ourselves on having grasped his previous point (108).

The above review shows that Donne's poetry has not been studied in the light of *dhvani* theory so far. The analysis of Donne's poetry from the perspective of Indian poetics, and especially *dhvani* theory, will reveal many hidden aspects which may help in understanding his concept of wit better.

III

Dhvani is embedded in almost all the poems of Donne but it can be admired only by the *sahridaya* reader. John Donne's poems have two meanings: one is the *vāchya* or the overt meaning and the other is the *pratiyamāna* or implied meaning. Donne chooses those words, which mean more than the literal meaning. The artistic use of *vyanjanā* makes his poems great. According to Anandavardhana the poem having the dominance of *vyanjanā* can be considered a good poem. And Donne's poems are full of this quality. *Dhvani*-theory can be compared to Eliot's theory of Objective Correlative, Hopkin's Theory of Inscape and Roland Barthes's Textual Analysis. According to Barthes, textual analysis does not try to find out what determines the text, but rather how the texts explode.

The poem 'The Blossome' is addressed to a poor flower. The blossom is used as a symbol of love. Symbols are related with *dhvani*. Many times symbols in Donne's poetry convey such meanings which take the form of *dhvani* as per the concept of Indian Poetics.

The first stanza develops the imagery of the flower, its birth, growth and death. The persona addresses his beloved as a poor flower. But he does not mention the term beloved in the poem. The persona addresses his beloved, whom he has been watching and he is pleased with her development and growth for the last few days. His beloved is now mature and looks proud and beautiful like a flower standing on its stalk. The persona calls her a poor flower because her beauty is transient like that of a flower blasted by snow. After a short while, her youth will come to an end like a flower which fades and falls to the ground. The persona has been watching the flower as growing from its birth to maturity for six or seven days. In the case of the persona's beloved the period of time may be taken as several years. The persona reminds the flower that its freshness and beauty will not endure for a long time. The suggestion is that the flower or the lady of his love should be a source of joy to the persona as long as her beauty lasts. The persona does not bemoan the evanescence of youth and beauty, he suggestively implores the lady to be conscious of the fact that she will not be young and beautiful forever and so she should make it a point to give him whatever delight and joy that she is capable of giving now only.

> Little think'st thou, poore flower,
> Whom I have watch'd sixe or seaven dayes,
> And seene thy birth, and seene what every houre
> Gave to thy growth, thee to this height to raise,
> And now dost laugh and triumph on this bough,
> Little think'st thou
> That it will freeze anon, and that I shall
> Tomorrow finde thee falne, or not at all. (Lines 1-8)

The persona warns the beloved that though now she laughs at him, thinking that she has won a victory over persona's heart but she scarcely realizes the fact that her beauty will be frozen by the winter of age in near future. The persona implies that the youthful beauty of a woman is as transient as that of a flower.

So in the above stanza we can clearly find the suggestion of *avivaksitavācya dhvani* (unintended denotation) as here the primary expressed meaning or sense is not the one intended. It is based on *lakshanā* or indication. And here particularly *arthāntarsamkramittavācyadhvani* is used as here the expressed sense or the literal and primary meaning shifts into another sense or implied actual meaning. Here the persona has not used the word beloved anywhere but the word flower suggests the beloved. This is *pratiyamāna* or the implied meaning.

In the second stanza there is a suggestion of the persona's desire for an illicit sexual relationship with the lady whom he loved. The word forbidding is not a quibble; it suggests that the lady has declined the advances of the persona. The persona addresses his heart and declares that it is useless for the heart to pursue the beloved with affection. The lady will not make any favourable response to his heart because she is a forbidden tree i.e. a lady married to another man. She is also the forbidding tree because she has already discarded the advances of the persona. The persona addresses his own heart which hopes foolishly that by hovering around the flower, it may be able to embrace it. The above situation suggests that the persona is addressing his own heart as a bird which is trying to make a nest in the forbidden tree and taste the blossom at an appropriate time.

> Little think'st thou poore heart
> That labour'st yet to nestle thee,
> And think'st by hovering here to get a part
> In a forbidden or forbidding tree,
> And hop'st her stiffenesse by long seige to bow: (ll. 9-13)

The first two stanzas of this poem are a little ambiguous because the object addressed to has not been clearly explained. Six or seven days are a fairly long time to watch a flower from its birth to maturity but it is a short period for the growth of a woman. She is described as a flower of that tree as she is childless and if she would have a child she would have been regarded as a fruit and her child would have been regarded as the seed of the fruit.

Thus, in the second stanza *vivaksitanyaparāvācyadhvani* (extended denotation) is used. The primary expressed meaning is subordinate to the implied meaning i.e. along with the literal meaning something more is intended. This is based on *abidhā* or denotation. Here the expressive power of words conveys an extraordinary sense of beauty making the primary expressed meaning totally subordinate to the implied meaning. The persona compares his heart to a bird, the forbidden tree to the beloved's house and the blossom to the beloved.

'A Valediction: Forbidding Mourning' is a poem which excellently illustrates Donne's wit. The subject of this poem is that of the union of the lovers even when they are separated. In the opening line a comparison between the moment of dying and the moment of separation has been made. Separation is death of the lovers, during which their bodies become extinct and their souls get mixed. Separation, i.e. death, is however, not rejected but eagerly desired, because death or separation is not the end of their love. On the contrary, it leads to a richer expression of love. Lovers are compared to virtuous men who are not afraid of death. On the contrary, virtuous men wish that death should better come sooner than later because they regard death as a gateway to eternal life. Death takes the virtuous men to an infinitely richer life which the common people are ignorant of.

The persona says that the true lovers are like virtuous men who are also ready to get separated i.e. to die in order that they might attain the higher union of souls. The suggestion in these lines is that only worldly-minded people are sad on dying whereas virtuous men are not afraid of death. Here the persona persuades his unhappy wife not to feel grief at his going abroad. He gives an argument in support of his advice. He says that when righteous men are dying some of their sad friends are filled with sorrow. Some other friends, who are unhappy, burst into exclamations of sorrow. They wish their dear ones on death bed should not die and leave them. But the virtuous men are calm and quiet. They say goodbye to life calmly and signal their souls to leave, and breathe their last peacefully. Even so the persona and his wife should take leave of each other, when he goes abroad. The persona implies that both of them are virtuous that is righteous and spiritual lovers. So they stand on a higher level than that on which lovers of physical beauty stand.

> As virtuous men passe mildly away,
> And whisper to their soules, to goe,
> Whilst some of their sad friends doe say,
> The breath goes now, and some say, no. (ll. 1-4)

The poem "A Valediction: Forbidding Mourning" is full of intellectual poetic wit. The theme of the poem is subtle. The persona indirectly tells his unhappy wife that spiritual love is something divine and holy. It is quite independent of the body. So the two spiritual lovers can never feel the pain of physical separation from each other. Their souls are invisibly connected with each other by the ties of spiritual love. Physically they keep each other in mind constantly. When one of them is physically away from the other, they are present in each other's mind; so there is constant mental unity of the two. There is a blending of passion, thought, feeling and reason in this poem.

In the above stanza *vivaksitanyaparāvācyadhvani* (extended denotation) is used; the primary expressed meaning is intended but it is subordinate to the implied meaning i.e. along with the literal meaning something more is intended. This is based on *abidhā* or denotation. Here the expressive power of words conveys an extraordinary sense of beauty making the primary expressed meaning totally subordinate to the implied meaning. The narrator wants to make his beloved understand that their love is spiritual and not physical and they cannot be separated even after death. Here *samlaksyakramavyangya dhvani* is used as the suggested meaning is of perceptible process. Here *alankār-dhvani* is used as the main meaning is suggested by a figure of speech, which is a poetic embellishment (*alankāra*). And here the persona has compared the lover to virtuous men.

In the context of Anandvardhana *dhvani theory*, the last three stanzas of this poem convey more than the literal meaning. The spiritual love between the lovers is suggested by the comparison of their souls to a pair of compass on the one hand; on the other, it successfully conveys the sense of a stirred heart burdened with emotions arising at the time of departure of a lover from his beloved. The image of compass illustrates a point already proved; the perfect blending of the two souls in a higher, spiritual love unattainable by common ordinary men and women. The soul of the beloved is likened to the fixed foot of the compass, because she is staying at home. The narrator going to a foreign land is the other foot which moves apart. The fixed foot may seem to be unmoving, yet it does lean towards the other foot moving away.

The last section of the poem has suggestion that just as the circle is completed at the same point from where it started, the persona will return to his beloved to find her as much in love with him as she was in love when he left her.

In this stanza the difference between the real love and sensual desire has been brought out by means of the image of compass. The persona argues that even if the souls of the lovers are two, they are one in reality. Just as the two legs of the compass are separate but united at the top, in the same way, the lovers are united even in separation because they continue to have intense longing for each other. The lovers are united spiritually even when they are separate physically. The lover may go out for some time, but he is bound to return home, just as the moving foot of the compass returns to the center after completing the circle.

If they be two, they are two so
As stiffe twin compasses are two,
Thy soule the fixt foot, makes no show
To move, but doth, if the' other doe.

And though it in the centre sit,
Yet when the other far doth rome,
It leanes, and hearkens after it,

> And growes erect, as that comes home.
> Such wilt thou be to mee, who must
> Like th' other foot, obliquely runne;
> Thy firmnes makes my circle just,
> And makes me end, where I begunne. (ll. 25-36)

The image of the compass is a symbol to represent the unity of two souls which are abstract things. Evidently, this image is the instrument of his wit to represent his poetic perception and his special insight. He believed that in the universe, all things stood in fundamental relation to one another. The comparison is a literal one but to the *sahridaya* reader it is fantastic, and to an unpoetic mind it is of no worth. Here also *vivaksitanyaparāvācyadhvani* (extended denotation) is used, the expressive power of words conveys an extraordinary sense of beauty making the primary expressed meaning totally subordinate to the implied meaning. As here basically the persona wants to make his beloved understand that their love is spiritual and not physical and they cannot be separated even after death. Here the *samlaksyakramavyangyadhvani* is used as the suggested meaning is of perceptible process. Here *alankāra-dhvani* is used as the main meaning is suggested by a figure of speech. Thus, by the use of *dhvani* (suggestion), the poem assumes significance. *Dhvani* directs the readers to meanings beyond the text.

The *dhvani* concept, in fact, covers all aspects of literary art; for by concentrating on the suggestive element, both writer and reader are engaged with the literary beauties. In fact, almost all features of Indian Poetics, i.e. *Rasa, Alankāra, Dhvani* etc., can be observed in the poetry of John Donne. In the present paper his poems have been analyzed in the background of *dhvani*-theory.

Works Cited

Ansari, A.A., ed. *Essays on John Donne.* Aligarh Muslim Univ., 1974.

Bennet, Joan. *Five Metaphysical Poets*. Cambridge UP, 1964.

Booth, Roy, ed. *The Collected Poems of John Donne*. Wordsworth Poetry Library, 2002.

Chandra, Naresh. *John Donne and Metaphysical Poetry*. Doaba, 1991.

Dwivedi, Shiv Prasad. *Dhvanyāloka of Sri Anandavardhanācharya.* Chaukhambha, 2013.

Gardner, Helen, Introduction. *The Metaphysical Poets*. OUP, 1967.

_____, ed. *John Donne: The Elegies and the Songs and Sonnets.* Oxford UP, 1965.

Grierson, H.J.C., ed. *Donne: Poetical Works*.1933.

_____. "Metaphysical Poetry" *Seventeenth Century English Poetry: Modern Essays in Criticism*, ed. William R. Keast. OUP, 1962.

_____, ed. *The Poems of John Donne* 2 vols. OUP, 1912.

Guibbory, Achsah, ed. *The Cambridge Companion to John Donne*. Cambridge UP, 2006.

Krishnamoorthy, K. *Dhvanyāloka*. Karnataka University, 1974.

Labriola, Albert C. Style, "Wit and Prosody in the Poetry of John Donne," *Oxford Handbook of John Donne*. ed. Jeanne Shami, et al. Oxford UP, 2011.

Lewis, C.S. "Donne and Love Poetry in the Seventeenth Century." *The Love Poetry of John Donne.* 1938.

Lovelock, Julian, ed. *Donne: Songs and Sonnets*. Macmillan, 1973.

Raja, K. Kunjunni. *Anandavardhana*. Sahitya Akademi, 1995.

Roston, Murray. *The Soul of Wit: A Study of John Donne.* OUP, 1974.

Saintsbury, George. "John Donne." *John Donne: A Collection of Critical Essays*, ed. Helen Gardner. Prentice Hall of India, 1979.

Sanders, Wilbur. *John Donne's Poetry*. Cambridge UP, 1971.

Sharma, Mukunda Madhava. *The Dhvani Theory in Sanskrit Poetics.* Chowkhamba Sanskrit Series, 1968.

_____. *John Donne: The Critical Heritage*. Routledge and Kegan Paul, 1975.

Walimbe, Y.S. *Abhinavagupta on Indian Aesthetics*. Ajanta P, 1980.

Spiritual and Secular Strains in the Poetry of Swami Vivekananda

JAGDISH BATRA
O.P. Jindal Global University, Sonepat

Most people in India know Swami Vivekananda as a great spiritual leader of modern India who made the world conscious of the rich spiritual wealth of this country. He was successful in bringing about a sea-change in the outlook of the common Westerner towards Hinduism which was hitherto looked upon as nothing more than a lot of voodoo and primitive mysticism. Whereas some of the ancient texts had already been accessed by the scholars of Europe and America, the ordinary mortals there had only now the opportunity to see in flesh and blood an Indian mystic. As is common knowledge now, Swamiji's powerful oratory and writings were noticed and admired after he addressed the World Religions Conference in Chicago in 1893.

There is no denying the fact that Swami Vivekananda's prose writings continue to be enjoyed and admired even now. His place in English literature produced by Indians is secure on that count, more so as he belongs to a period when this literature was in a nascent stage. What is missing is the recognition of Swami Vivekananda as a poet also. This article aims to focus on Swamiji as a poet.

Swamiji's poems mark an important step in the evolution of English poetry produced by Indians. The era of Indo-Anglian poetry, as the genre was known earlier, is supposed to have begun with Henry Derozio's poems (Iyengar 34). After this, Michael

Madhusudan Dutt published his *Voices of the Past* in 1848 and the *Dutt Family Album* appeared in 1870. Toru Dutt, the prodigal child of this family, had her *A Sheaf Gleaned in French Fields* published in 1875 in England. Most of Swamiji's poems appear between 1895 and 1898. The output is not very large—only 45 pieces including some translated from Swamiji's earlier Bengali and Sanskrit verses, but the poems have a rare beauty. These poems are found in scattered form in *The Complete Works of Swami Vivekananda*.

Swamiji's poetry is born of various moods and dispositions. The poems reflect spiritual ecstasy, philosophical musings, motivational suggestions, personal anguish and lively interaction with acquaintances. "The Song of the Sanyasin," an early piece composed in July 1895, beautifully imparts the Vedantic message. A Sanyasin, i.e., an ascetic is called upon to continue his march on the road leading from 'I' to 'all,' cancelling out all distinctions and divisions.

> Know, slave is slave, caressed or whipped, not free
> For fetters though of gold, are not strong to bind;
> Then off with them, Sanyasin bold! Say
> "Om Tat Sat, Om!"

The urgings find echo in the testimony of Sister Christine. Writing about the spiritual disposition of the Swami those days, she remarks: "Then he would rush up to one of us with blazing eyes and finger pointing and would exclaim, 'Remember, God is the only reality.'" (168) One cannot miss the Browning touch in the following lines. It is not merely the short and crisp phrases that remind us of Browning but also his obscurity that seems a part of Swamiji's verse:

> Heed them no more how body lives or goes
> Its task is done, let Karma float it down;
> Let one put garlands on, another kick
> This frame; say naught.

In "Peace," written in 1899, Swamiji's description of peace turns mystical. The sheer beauty of these quatrains is irresistible:

It is joy that never spoke
And grief unfelt, profound
Immortal life unlived.
Eternal death unmourned. . . .
It is song that lives unsung
And knowledge never known.

The mystic strain is present in the poem "To Kali the Mother" which appears to have been written in an ecstatic state. Iyengar rightly calls it an "almost apocalyptic vision of the breaking of the worlds and Dance of Doom." (52)

The sea has joined the fray,
And swirls up mountain-waves,
To reach the pitchy sky,
The flash of lurid light
Reveals on every side
A thousand, thousand shades
Of Death begrimed and black—
Scattering plagues and sorrows,
Dancing mad with joy.
Come, Mother, come!

Similar sentiments can be seen in another poem titled "And Let Shyama dance there," also written originally in Bengali. Shyama stands for Kali in this poem which, using a rich imagery, depicts clash of elements having bright and dark shades. Away from the horrid images of goddess Kali in the aforesaid two poems is "The Hymn of Creation" again rendered from Bengali, which is a beautiful mix of philosophical elucidation and poetic description. As the title suggests, it is a vision of creation as observed by a Yogi.

One mass, devoid of form, name and colour,
Timeless, devoid of time past and future,
Spaceless, voiceless, boundless, devoid of all—
Where rests hushed even speech of negation,

From thence, down floweth the river causal.

Incidentally, there is an English rendering of the *Nasadiya Sukta* from Rig Veda done by Swamiji and it bears the same title viz. "The Hymn of Creation." This theme is repeated in "The Hymn of Samadhi." There are other hymns dedicated for example, to Ramakrishna, to the Divine Mother and to Shiva (originally written in Sanskrit). "A Song I sing to thee" is the lengthiest hymn to "thee" that is explained as both *Purusha* and *Prakriti* (male and female principles) together. The poet is filled with wonder and awe at the interplay of the primal forces in the present moment as also at the time of doom. The burden of Vedantic philosophy makes the poem obscure and complex.

Reverting from these poems to the ones written in English, we have "Angles Unawares" consisting of three sections and marking the triumph of experience over the received word. It celebrates a ray of hope evinced by one given for long to misery, though the sage calls it superstition. The reverse is also possible with one brought up on luxuries taking the world for his own self only. His selfishness leads to an unfeeling heart that cannot feel joy. The quester welcomes misery as blessed because it relates him to the sea of humanity around him. The importance of feelings is effectively underlined here. Then, the unsavoury incidents of life which the world dubs as fall can fortunately open the eyes of an easy-go-lucky fellow to the newness of life. By wading through the sea of struggles can one reach "Peace Eternal." It reminds the reader of Swamiji's explication of Lord Krishna's message to Arjuna that he won't attain Moksha by shunning the world. The poem uses the image of a whirl to describe the maddening course of the worldly life. It is also full of figures like "surging waves" for the frets of life and transferred epithets like "dismal path." A racy verse is employed that reminds one of the oratorical skill of the Swami.

The poem "To the Awakened India" written primarily for *Prabuddha Bharat*, the journal of the Brotherhood founded by

Swamiji, is a powerful call to his motherland, the land of "cloud belted snows," to give up dreaming and resume her march "with gentle feet that would not break the/ Peaceful rest, even of the roadside dust." The Vedantic philosophy, however, finds its place here also:

> This is the land of dreams, where Karma
> Weaves enthreaded garlands with our thoughts
> Of flowers sweet or noxious, and none
> Has root or stem, being born in naught, which
> The softest breath of Truth drives back to
> Primal nothingness.

And yet man must face the reality, the "kinetic aspect" of which has been called Maya (Siddheshwaranand 335). Even love and service are described as "truer dreams"—dreams these are in any case. In "The Living God," Swamiji castigates worldly people for neglecting the living God: "He who is in you and outside you,/ Who works through all hands . . . He who is at once the high and the low,/ The sinner and the saint." This comprehensive definition of the living God subsuming all types of human beings is represented in common spiritual parlance as *Nar-Narayan*.

The poem "Hold on a while, brave heart," though in the vein of auto-suggestion, has an impersonal message also. Couched in the fourteen-syllabic line of the ballad, it calls for action: "Not a work will be lost, no struggle vain/ Though hopes be blighted, powers gone/ Of thy loins shall come the heirs to all." This stress on being bold in action "after such knowledge," as Eliot would have it, is something that distinguishes Swami Vivekananda from the other sages of the mainstream Hinduism. His uniqueness lies in interpreting Vedanta in a way that does not take away the usefulness of action in this world. He often called upon the youth to build muscles in the playfield than worry about heaven and hell. Very pertinently and poignantly, he asked, "What is the ideal of religion, then if this cannot be practical? And it certainly, cannot be. What are we here for? We are here for freedom, for knowledge. We want to know to make ourselves free. That is our life: one universal cry for freedom."

A fair portion of Swamiji's poetry deals with nature as backdrop, rather a prop for his philosophical musings. One such beautiful poem forms part of a letter written by Swamiji on Sept. 4, 1893 to one "Adhyapakji." It was Prof. J.H. Wright whom Swamiji addressed lovingly in this manner. There are quite a few letters exchanged between the two before some misunderstanding developed due to the machinations of some jealous Indian detractors of Swamiji. The poem in iambic pentameter is a captivating piece that reminds one of Wordsworth in the opening line of his famous poem on daffodils: "O'r Hill and dale and mountain range." The poem relates how the search for the Almighty leads one from the external world to the inner world, but this search is dependent not upon one's efforts but squarely upon the will of God. The quester tries all routes, is ultimately pitied upon by the Lord and one day he hears Him calling "My Son, my Son." Having had a glimpse of the divinity once, now even the external world of sights and sounds becomes a manifestation of Him. His grace provides him support in moments of weakness and desperation.

The poem "To an early Violet" is an allegorical one that has a pen picture of a pretty flower symbolizing the self:

> What though thy bed be frozen earth,
> Thy cloak the chilling blast
> What though no mate to cheer thy path,
> Thy sky with gloom o'ercast.

Swamiji's description of nature is captivating. This as well as another poem titled "To my own Soul" are meant to boost the spirit facing a callous world. Apart from the poems describing his philosophy, there are quite a few which are personal in nature. "Requiescat in Pace" (meaning May he rest in peace!) is written in memoriam to J.J. Goodwin, whose sweet remembrance is expected to fill his place in this world like "altar roses." For once, the poet in Vivekananda takes over the Vedantist in "To a Friend," originally written in Bengali. The poet rues the devious ways of the world. On the basis of personal experience, he finds: "The nobler is your heart, know for certain/ The more must be your share of misery." Swamiji rejects all formalism in religion and extols the virtue of all-embracing love without any expectation.

A bunch of poems covered under the title 'An Interesting Correspondence' in Part VIII of *The Complete Works of Swami Vivekananda* is addressed to Mary Hale, daughter of Mrs. and Mr. Hale, whom Swamiji light-heartedly addressed as Father Pope and Mother Church. The family was very intimate with him. The opening poem begins like a limerick: "Now sister Mary/ You need not be sorry," but soon we are treated to some fine quatrains with rhythmic movement of a ballad encapsulating pearls of wisdom:

> The beauteous earth, the glorious sun,
> The calm sweet moon, the spangled sky,
> Causation's laws do make them run;
> They live in bonds, in bonds they die.

We also have an exchange of doggerels. In one such piece, Miss Mary hints at the imperfection of the Swami's metre: "In thought and word, he could well beat her/ What bothered him though was the metre." Later, Swamiji has a jibe at her understanding of his message, through reference to the well-known anecdote in which the devotees show their ignorance about the identities of Rama and Sita well after the discourse on the *Ramayana* is over. The problem related to Mary's incomprehension of what she called "Eastern logic" about the real self and *Maya*. Swamiji's affection for the little girl and his insistence that she understand the concept takes a playful turn in another doggerel:

> Though many a lay her muse can bray
>   And play piano too,
> Her heart so cool, chills as a rule

The fool who comes to woo.

Of the poems personal in nature the one titled 'No one to blame' is a rare piece in which the poet reprimands the self for seeking to choose pleasure without welcoming the pain that follows it like its shadow. His spirits have ebbed to a point where his thirst for life is gone, leading him to desire eternal death. Out of this morass, only the grace of his Guru can extricate for which he prays in the last stanza. In "My Play is Done," we come across the anxiety of the poet over his failure to get a glimpse of the transcendental life. Calling upon the "Mother" to have pity on him, his tormented self cries:

> You sent me out in the dark to play, and wore a frightful mask;
> Then hope departed, terror came, and play became a task.
> Tossed to and fro, from wave to wave in this seething, surging sea
> Of passions strong and sorrows deep, grief *is*, and joy *to be*.

Swamiji also wrote a beautiful poem dedicated to American independence. Titled "To the Fourth of July," it shows Swamiji had high hopes from America much like Whitman and Thoreau. It is interesting to note that if Swamiji made an impact on America, he, in turn, was also impressed by the American love for freedom. It could not have been otherwise for a Sanyasin who found his motherland in shackles of slavery. In this poem, he looks upon America as the fruit of labours and sacrifices of the early settlers who "gave up home and love of friends." He calls upon her to move on and spread the light of liberty in the world. It is another matter that with the passage of time these fond hopes were belied.

The group of poems titled "The Dance of Shiva," "Shiva in Ecstasy," "To Shri Krishna," originally written in Bengali or Hindi, portray images of gods. Similarly, two hymns written in Sanskrit are sung in praise of Swamiji's Guru Ramakrishna Paramhans. Apart from these, Swamiji also translated Sanskrit verses from Shankaracharya, Bhartrihari, Vedas and Upanishads. "Who knows How Mother Plays" is a short elegant piece which dwells on the inscrutable ways of divinity. Only Mother's child is privileged to have a fleeting glimpse of this mysterious realm:

> What law would freedom bind?
> What merit guide her will,
> Whose freak is the greatest order,
> Whose will resistless law?

Swami Vivekananda's poetry is a vehicle of his thoughts and experiences. He wanted that "abstract Vedanta must become living—poetic—in everyday life" (Nehru 337). He stood for fearlessness, freedom, service and practical religion rather than any dogmas or rituals. His love for nature, his concern for the downtrodden and his faith in the dignity of man mark him as one of the foremost humanists of our times. S. Radhakrishnan, the philosopher President of India, rightly remarks: "Swami Vivekananda affirmed the universality of the spirit, the universality of all religions" (166) Here is poetry in the service of highest ideals of mankind.

Works Cited

Christine, Sister. "Memories of Swami Vivekananda." *Vedanta for the Modern Man,* ed. Christopher Isherwood. New York: Collier Books, 1962.

Iyengar, K.R. Srinivasa. *Indian Writing in English.* New Delhi: Sterling, 1985, reprint 1995.

Nehru, Jawaharlal. *Discovery of India.* New Delhi: Jawaharlal Nehru Memorial Fund/Oxford University Press 2003, Impression XXVIII.

President Radhakrishnan's Speeches and Writings. Publications Division, Ministry of Information and Publication, Govt. of India. May 1962-May1964.

Swami Siddheshwaranand, "A Hindu View of Christian Theology." *Vedanta for Modern Man*, ed. Christopher Isherwood. New York: Collier Books, 1962.

The Complete Works of Swami Vivekananda, Calcutta: Advait Ashram, 1955.

The Short Story in Hindi: Traditions and Trends

URVASHI SABU
PGDAV College, University of Delhi

> A young boy of fifteen went to a brothel and asked the prostitute, "Will I get a students' concession?" A forgotten expression shone briefly on the countenance of the middle-aged woman. She patted him gently on the shoulder and replied, "Why not son?" (Paul 51)

From the ancient Indian stories of the *Panchtantra* and the oral traditions of anecdotes to this pregnant four-line vignette of the contemporary world, the Indian short story has travelled a vast distance. There has hardly ever been a time in Indian literature when short stories did not occupy a prominent place. Episodes and stories from the *Ramayana*, the *Mahabharata* and the various Puranas have been told and retold along with the cycle of stories from the Jatakas, *Panchtantra*, *Hitopadesh* and *Vikramaditya and Betal*. The corpus increased with the contact with the Perso-Arabic world. Stories from the Middle-East like the Arabian Nights, Alif Laila etc. became a valuable part of Indian literature.

The short story as a genre however appeared in Indian literature when these mythological, adventurous and marvellous stories had exhausted their possibilities and the novel was firmly established. The distinctiveness of the genre can be identified through the various nomenclatures for the short story: 'katha,' 'akhyan,' 'upakhyan,' 'dastan,' 'afsana' etc. (Das 1991: 303)

As Sisir Kumar Das observes, "There are at least three distinct stages in the growth of the short story as a modern literary genre. Though autonomous, these stages are interrelated. The first stage is that of anecdotes and the second that of tales and fables. The third stage emerged in the 19th century with the advent of journals and periodicals which encouraged the growth of character sketches and reportage of incidents. There was yet another stage which belonged to the novella or short fiction. The short story, distinct from all the forms mentioned above, figures at the last stage of the evolution of narratives. Though it shares certain common features with these forms, it developed its own distinctiveness, characterized by the presence of a conscious narrative, foregrounding a particular incident, situation or a moment of emotional intensity." (*Ibid.* 302)

2

The development of the short story in Hindi owes a great deal to the ascendency of the periodical press. Indeed the Hindi short story is entirely the gift of the 20th century; appearing first in the monthly magazine *Saraswati* in 1900, thereafter in periodicals such as *Indu*, *Sapta-Saroj*, *Hans*. By the 1930s, a large number of literary periodicals in Hindi published stories by contemporary writers, many of whom made their foray into short story writing from writing novels and poetry, to cater to the demands of a reading public that preferred a complete story to the novels serialized in magazines and periodicals. The interesting part of the development of the Hindi short story is that for one, it has been the forte of poets and prose writers alike, and second, its myriad facets cannot be constrained or explained within the tenets of the Western concepts of story-telling. The Hindi short story neither follows fixed rules of progression, nor does it restrict itself to a single emotion or sensibility or even a detailed description of character. What it does have however is a conscious unity of circumstance, made poignant by the confluence of numerous emotions. As Das points out, "In some ways, the (Hindi) short story acts as a balance between historical novels and the novels dealing with social problems by identifying a new zone of experience. The growth of the short story also coincided with the growth of the new lyric (*Adhunik kavita)* which gave new meaning and significance to the commonplace things in nature and life. The short story learnt from the lyric the art of compactness of form and the unity of emotion. It followed the narrative techniques of the novel, but eventually it discovered its true nature by establishing its relationship with the lyric." (*Ibid.* 307)

While early Hindi short stories are realistic or romantic in the main, they have a moral bias. Kishorilal Goswami's "Indumati" (1900) is a love story set against a historical background; Madhav Rao Sapre's "Ek Tokri Bhar Mitti" (1901) is the story of the conflict between a poor widow and her wealthy landlord. Ramchandra Shukla's "Gyarah Varsh Ka Samay" (1903) is the glorification of the Indian concept of marital love and Chandradhar Sharma Guleri's "Usne Kaha Tha" (1915) is a story of love and sacrifice illuminated by idealism. A study of the initial developmental stages of the structure of the Hindi short story reveals that the love stories of the earlier years contain neither the minuteness nor the nuanced development of the later stories. Their aim was primarily, in the Horatian sense, to instruct and entertain. They convey a sense of social inclusivity that inclines towards both idealism and realism.

The Hindi short story really began to develop in 1916 when Munshi Premchand switched from writing in Urdu to writing in Hindi. Indeed, Premchand is the colossus that strides across the pillars of the Hindi and the Urdu short story, enriching both with his works. With the emergence of Premchand on the literary scene, the Hindi short story, as Bhisham Sahni points out, `moved out of the narrow sphere of personal relations and entered the larger sphere of social life, of social problems and of the destiny of the people as a whole.' (Das 1995: 269)

The publication of Premchand's "Panch Parmeshwar" in 1916 heralded the onset of a new age in the history of the Hindi short story. His repertoire of more than 300 short stories is collected in eight volumes of *Mansarovar*. His stories, like his novels, are intricately connected with the Indian village. He wrote on all kinds of themes: psychological, social, character-oriented, historical, political and domestic. The middle class and the rural peasantry occupy a central position in his stories. He has left no sphere of middle-class existence untouched. Incompatible marriages, widow remarriage, prostitution, drunkenness, the decline of the joint family system, capitalist exploitation, bourgeois psychology, economic disparity, problems of agriculture, peasant-landlord relations, the moneylender culture, lack of unity and a life devoid of values and self-esteem as the primary causes of the inequities of existence, rise of nationalism, moral upliftment, decline of socialism and the hypocrisies of religion all form the vast kaleidoscopic canvas of his stories. Stories like "Udhaar," a protest against the dowry system; "Nairashya," that criticizes the social preference for a male child to a girl child; "Sudra," about the miserable existence of an untouchable who has a beautiful daughter; "Poos ki Raat," the story of an impoverished peasant shivering through a freezing January night; or Sadgati, a terrifying story of the cruelty of man to man are examples of his art and vision.

Premchand's linguistic style is endearing for its straight forward simplicity and brevity of expression in thought, emotion and figurative language. He wrote with a 'detached involvement,' in a narrative voice cold and sarcastic yet keenly observant. He couched his idealism in realism and used irony as his most powerful stylistic technique.

> One Holi morning, Pandit Moteram Shastri—that devotee of pastries and lover of sweets—sat on a broken cot in his courtyard, his head hanging low, the very image of care and melancholy. His faithful spouse sat nearby watching him anxiously and trying in her gentle voice to wheedle him out of his depression.

Thus begins "Manushya ka Param Dharm," bare, precise, ironical. "Kafan," published in 1936, is one of the last stories of Premchand and arguably his masterpiece. It is the story of the total dehumanization of man caused by poverty and deprivation. Ghisu and Madhav, numbed and deadened by years of hunger, voraciously devour roasted potatoes stolen from a field even as Madhav's pregnant wife Budhiya screams in the agony of labour inside their ramshackle cottage. The morning finds her dead, flies buzzing over her contorted face, the baby dead in her womb. Now begins the task of procuring a shroud for the unfortunate woman. Both father and son beg from door to door for money for the shroud managing to collect the princely sum of five rupees. Faced with the cold realization that a shroud is nothing but a piece of cloth that will burn away with the corpse, father and son spend the entire sum on a full meal (the one they last remember eating was 20 years ago at the Thakur's wedding) and on drinking themselves into a frenzied hysteria. Bereavement, sorrow, guilt, social customs and religious rituals all pale into insignificance before this naked dance of hunger and deprivation. 'Then they started to dance. They jumped and sprang, fell back, twisted, gesticulated, mimed, and finally they collapsed dead drunk right there' (Premchand 57). According to R.D. Mishra, "The world of Premchand is more vivid, animated and varied than that of any other story writer in Hindi. His stories are primarily anecdotal, dealing with situations or incidents, but the sub-text is always human and humane. He locates his characters in the midst of situational conflicts and reveals their innermost secrets. His stories are studies in psychology, primarily the psychology of the conscious mind, made unique by his individual style." (Qtd. Rajpal 410)

The other pillar of the Premchand era is Jaishankar Prasad. His 69 stories are collected in *Chhaya*, *Pratidhwani*, *Akaashdeep*, *Aandhi* and *Indrajeet*. His stories unfold in an expression that is steeped in Indian culture. The compassion of Buddhism, the glorious past of India, selfless sacrifice, generosity of character and idealism permeate his consciousness and emerge in his stories clothed in poetic beauty and imaginative ecstasy, relegating the preacher to the background. Instead of an explicit or implied moral, there is a sensitive and emotional tension at the conclusion. Prasad's style brought about a magnitudinal change in the linguistics of the Hindi short story. According to Girish Rastogi, "Prasad's stories connect not so much with the external material social world as with the vicissitudes, dilemmas and emotions of the human heart. . . . His stories are lyrical, emotional expressions of man's internal world." (*Ibid.* 418)

The period after Premchand from 1936 onwards witnessed far reaching change in the art and science of story-telling and saw the emergence of new streams. Writers that carried forward the tradition of Premchand such as Yashpal, Rangeya Raghav, Upendranath Ashk and Bhagwaticharan Verma were more or less influenced by Marxist ideology. Motivated by social consciousness, they based their stories on the conflicts of materialism. Another stream of writers such as Ilachandra Joshi, Jainendra and Satchidanand Hiranand Vatsyayan 'Agyeya' were influenced by the psychoanalytical techniques of Freud, Adler and Jung. Thus, Marxism and Freudian psychoanalysis were the chief influences on the Hindi short story of the post-Independence era. Following are some of the trends in short story writing to have gained currency since then.

New Story (*Nai Kahaani)*: Although beset with debate regarding its nomenclature, this phenomenon found expression around 1956 at about the same time that New Poetry was making its presence felt. The New Story is inspired by Marxism and Existentialism. It is unique in its amalgamation of socialist tendencies with a commitment to articulate human truths. It portrays contemporary Indian society in a state of flux and stresses on the role of economic changes in the transformations coming over the domestic sphere. Love stories comprise a major chunk of the New Story. These are not just ordinary tales of love but tragedies conveying the entire gamut of emotions emerging from situational tensions, complexities and the conflicts between morality and passion that arise out of changing contexts. The pillars of the New Story are Mohan Rakesh, Rajendra Yadav and Kamleshwar. Dharmvir Bharti's "Gulki Banno" and Mannu Bhandari's "Sazaa" are some examples of the New Story.

Anti-story (*Akahaani*): Nihilism and paradox form the main themes of the Anti-story. The woman as wife becomes the object of anger and hatred. On the one hand, this destroys traditional notions of purity, chastity and devotion to the husband and on the other it questions the very sanctity of marriage. The voice of negation is prominent in the Anti-story. It not only negates traditional values, it violently undermines the very existence of values in literature. The Anti-story presents contradiction, agony, loneliness, disintegration and the death wish as terrifying realities of existence. It is against plot development or story of any kind. It presents a series of disconnected scenes, much like real life and believes that nothing in life either begins or ends with art. Some of the writers of this genre are Prayag Shukla, Ramesh Bakshi (*Pita Dar Pita)*, Dudhnath (*Iceberg),* Ravinder Kaalia (*Black Register)*.

Conscious Story (*Sachetan Kahaani*): Taking its name from the Activist Movement in story writing in France and Germany, this genre opposes the mannerisms of the New Story and tries to rescue the Hindi story from the valuelessness and individualistic emphasis of the Anti-story. According to the founder of the magazine *Sachetan*, Dr. Maheep Singh, "The Conscious story presents a perspective from which life can be lived and life *wants* to be lived. Since man naturally tends towards life, consciousness is an active life generating force. It realizes that the conscious, the subconscious and the unconscious all play a crucial role in the making of man's personality" (*Ibid.* 425). The conscious story presents man as fully aware of his helplessness and struggling to escape from it. It depicts the disintegration of human relationships and values in urban life. This disintegration neither angers nor agonizes man any more. Sexual relations are portrayed as being consumed with profound agony. At the centre is man, striving to liberate himself from this anguish. Simplicity is the defining feature of this genre; its central ground is the changing value systems of middle-class existence. Krishna Baldev Vaid's *Laapata* and Kuldeep Bagga's *Freezer Mein Lage Sambandh* are some examples of this genre.

Parallel Story (*Samantar Kahaani*): Popularized by Kamleshwar through his magazine *Sarika* (1972-1978), the Parallel story as its name suggests, runs on two parallel lines. It calls for the emancipation of man from the forces that compel him to live in a strangulatory environment where even his basic needs are not met. At the same time, it hits out ruthlessly against the weak links which debilitate man's struggle against those forces. Struggle and effort emerge as values in these stories that portray the realities of lower and middle-class existence. They do not turn a blind eye to the decline of values like respect, reverence, and sympathy. These values are often reflected in the stories in generation gaps and incompatibilities. They adopt a healthy approach towards sexual relations. Kamleshwar's "Bayaan" is one example of the Parallel Story.

Active Story (*Sakriya Kahaani*): Using a term borrowed from the western concept of the active story, writer Rakesh Vatsa used this nomenclature as a slogan in his periodical *Manch* (1978-79). The Active Story portrays man's conscious energy and vitality, his cognition and understanding that emancipate him from helplessness and intellectual impotency, enable him to challenge his own weaknesses and ultimately to stand up against the forces that defy change. These stories are dedicated to the positive role of literature in bridging the chasm between intention and effort, thought and action. Virendra Mendiratta, Chitra Mudgal, Ramesh Batra are some of the writers associated with this movement.

Marxist Story (*Marxwadi Kahaani*): An extended version of the Progressive Movement, this genre takes the help of Marxist ideology to emphasize class struggle as the only means to rid society of corruption, injustice, exploitation and dishonesty. Most Marxist stories are political. Rarely do romantic or domestic themes figure in this genre. A number of writers associated with the Parallel or Active story were subsumed within this movement. From 1982 onwards, Marxist stories appeared in journals such as *Kalam*, *Kathan*, *Uttargatha*, *Uttarraardh*. Ramesh Upadhyaya, Asgar Vajahat, Surendra Menon and Namita Singh are some of the writers in this genre.

Contemporary Short story (*Samkaaleen Laghu Katha)*: This is the latest buzzword, which includes almost all the above classifications in some form or the other. Eschewing moral values and instruction (the features of the traditional short story), the story today has attached itself to the woes and tribulations of the common man. It presents artistically the changes sweeping over personal, political and social life. Depth and profundity despite brevity of expression are the essence of the contemporary story.

Any discussion of the trends and traditions of the Hindi short story is incomplete without a mention of the unique contribution that women have made to this genre. Astonishingly enough, the first original short story in Hindi was written by a woman at the start of the 20th century. In 1907, Rajbala Ghosh, under the pseudonym Banga Mahila, wrote "Dulaiwali" which was published in Mahavir Prasad Dwivedi's *Saraswati*. It was this that opened the floodgates for story writing by women. Writers like Yashoda Devi, Priyamvada Devi, Usha Devi Mitra and Girija Devi wielded the pen to criticize social evils in their stories, conveying what they wanted to despite the absence of stylistic smoothness or linguistic excellence. But they were never taken seriously by established male writers of the time. Even a socially conscious and progressive writer like Premchand did not include any serious discussions on women writers in his literary periodicals *Hans*, *Sudha* or *Madhuri* despite the fact that his wife Shivrani Devi was herself a writer of short stories. The reasons for this neglect are not difficult to envisage in a patriarchal society, more so in a literary set up, dominated and controlled by male ideas of excellence and worth. However, strangulation sometimes results in a scream and not always in choked silence. The 30s and 40s saw an ever-increasing number of women writers who now began to express themselves unhesitatingly not just on the social, economic and domestic realities of their existence but also on intimate man-woman relations. Shivrani Devi, Chandraprabha Dwivedi, Manorama Sinha and Mahadevi Verma are some of the well-known writers of this period.

It is mystifying to note that despite making their presence felt on the literary scene, women writers were nowhere close to being incorporated in the literary canon. Even an established writer and critic like Acharya Ramchandra Shukla did not include women's writing in his *Hindi Sahitya ka Itihas* despite repeated revisions and editions. Notwithstanding the stepfatherly treatment, women's writing increased manifold as they began to understand the significance and contextuality of literature in their lives. They spoke about the plight of women exploited and suppressed for centuries. They witnessed the political contribution of women like Sarojini Naidu, Annie Besant, Vijayalakshmi Pandit, Kamla Nehru and Kasturba Gandhi. Jolted out of their limited themes pertaining to social and domestic life, they now began to be connected with the larger issues of the nation and the world.

The Partition transformed not just the nation but women's writing as well. Writers like Krishna Sobti, Shivani, Mannu Bhandari, Rajni Panikker and Prakashwati Narayan came forward with astounding creative energy to evocatively express the multiple facets of the modern woman in their short stories. They touched upon the hitherto undiscussed aspects of womanhood with candour, realistically charting the course of changing man-woman relations, families and concepts of sexual morality.

The latter half of the 20th century has been full of possibilities for women's writing. Although Nirmal Verma's *Parindey* has been regarded as the harbinger of the New Story movement, Usha Priyamvada's *Waapsi* is considered equivalent. Coincidentally both were published in 1955. From the 1970s onwards, it has been impossible to ignore or marginalize women's writing. Staying away from literary camps, imbroglios and establishment battles, women short story writers like Mamta Kaalia, Mridula Sinha, Chitra Mudgal, Naseema Sharma, Usha Mahajan, Mridula Garg and Manisha Kulshreshtha have exposed the double standards and pseudo morality of society, accorded respect to the multiple roles of women as homemakers and professionals, and openly discussed changing social and sexual contexts.

3

In the last decades of the 20th century and the first decade of the 21st, the pressures of a rapidly changing world are visible on the short story. The good part is that modern short story writers do not succumb to the challenges posed by these changes. Rather they are using with greater dexterity the potent weapon of this genre. The reason for the longevity and lasting appeal of the short story is that it refuses to be straitjacketed into movements and formulae. It continues to delve into the life of the common man presenting it both realistically and imaginatively. It comments fearlessly on contemporary existence in all its material, psychological, social, economic and political aspects and continues to enthrall generations of readers who prefer its simplicity and brevity to the vastness of the novel or the density of the poem.

Works Cited

Batrohi. *Hindi Kahani ke Atharah Kadam.* Allahabad: Vibha Prakashan, 1990

Darpan, Mahesh, ed. *Sab Kuch Kareene Se: Beesvi Shatabdi ki Hindi Kahaniyan.* Vol. 11, New Delhi: Samyik Prakashan,2000

Das, Sisir Kumar. *A History of Indian Literature. 1800-1910 Western Impact, Indian Response*, Vol. VIII. New Delhi: Sahitya Akademi, 1991.

_____. *A History of Indian Literature, 1911-1956. Struggle for Freedom: Triumph and Tragedy*, Vol. IX. New Delhi: Sahitya Akademi, 1995.

Joshi, Himanshu, ed. *Shreshtha Samantar Kahaniyaan*. Delhi: Parag Prakashan,1976.

Premchand. "Kafan," *Shatabdi ki Kaljayi Kahaniyan*, ed. Kamleshwar. New Delhi: Kitabghar, 2010.

Kumar, Sudhindra. *Hindi Sahitya ka Itihas*. New Delhi: Kadambari Prakashan, 1999.

Narang, Sudershan, ed. *Shreshth Sachetan Kahaniyan*. Delhi: Sharda Prakashan,1978.

_____, ed. *Shreshth Janvadi Kahaniyan*. Hapur: Shirshak Prakashan, 1987.

Paul, Joginder. "Taal," *Samkaleen Bhartiya Laghu Kathayein*, ed. Sukesh Sahni. Delhi: Megha Books, 2008, p. 51. My translation.

Prasad, Jaishankar. *Prasad ki Shreshth Kahaniyan*. Delhi: Sahitya Pracharak,1989.

Rajpal, Hukumchand. *Hindi Sahitya ka Itihas*. New Delhi: Vikas, 1997.

Ramakrishnan, E.V., ed. *Indian Short Stories* (1900-2000). New Delhi: Sahitya Akademi, 2000.

Sahni, Sukesh, ed. *Samkaleen Bhartiya Laghu Kathayein*. Delhi: Megha Books, 2008.

Saraf, Ramkali, ed. *Samkaleen Hindi Katha Lekhikayein*. Varanasi: Anurag Prakashan,1977.

Snatak, Vijayendra. *Hindi Sahitya ka Itihas*. Delhi: Sahitya Akademi, 1996.

Shukla, Ramchandra. *Hindi Sahitya Ka Itihas*. Kanpur: Chandralok Prakashan, 2002.

Tiwari, Surendra, ed. *Beesvi Sadi ki Mahila Kathakaron Ki Kahaniyan*. New Delhi: Naman Prakashan, 2010.